WAYSIDE COURTSHIPS

HAMLIN GARLAND

1st WORLD
LIBRARY
Literary Society

Wayside Courtships

Hamlin Garland

© 1st World Library, 2007
PO Box 2211
Fairfield, IA 52556
www.1stworldlibrary.com
First Edition

LCCN: 2007934122

Softcover ISBN: 978-1-4218-9647-2
Hardcover ISBN: 978-1-4218-9747-9
eBook ISBN: 978-1-4218-9547-5

Purchase *"Wayside Courtships"*
as a traditional bound book at:
www.1stWorldLibrary.com/purchase.asp?ISBN=978-1-4218-9647-2

1st World Library is a literary, educational organization
dedicated to:

- Creating a free internet library of downloadable ebooks

- Hosting writing competitions and offering book publishing
scholarships.

1ˢᵗ World Library Literary Society

Giving Back to the World

"If you want to work on the core problem, it's early school literacy."

- James Barksdale, former CEO of Netscape

"No skill is more crucial to the future of a child, or to a democratic and prosperous society, than literacy."

- Los Angeles Times

"Literacy... means far more than learning how to read and write... The aim is to transmit... knowledge and promote social participation."

- UNESCO

"Literacy is not a luxury, it is a right and a responsibility. If our world is to meet the challenges of the twenty-first century we must harness the energy and creativity of all our citizens."

- President Bill Clinton

"Parents should be encouraged to read to their children, and teachers should be equipped with all available techniques for teaching literacy, so the varying needs and capacities of individual kids can be taken into account."

- Hugh Mackay

CONTENTS

AT THE BEGINNING

She was in the box; he was far above in the gallery.

He looked down and across and saw her sitting there fair as a flower and robed like a royal courtesan in flame and snow.

Like a red torch flamed the ruby in her hair. Her shoulders were framed in her cloak, white as marble warmed with firelight. Her gloved hands held an opera glass which also glowed with flashing light.

His face grew dark and stern. He looked down at his poor coat and around at the motley gallery which reeked with the smell of tobacco and liquor.

Students were there—poor like himself, but with great music-loving, hungry, ambitious souls. Men and women of refinement and indomitable will sat side by side with drunken loafers who had chanced to stumble up the stairway.

His eyes went back to her. So sweet and dainty was every thread on her fair body. No smell of toil, nor touch of care, nor mark of weariness. Her flesh was ivory, her eyes were jewels, her heart was as clean and sweet as her eyes. She was perfectly clothed, protected, at ease.

No, not at ease. She seemed restless. Again and again she swept her glass around the lower balcony.

The man in the gallery knew she was looking for him, and he took a bitter delight in the distance between them. He waited, calm as a lion in his power.

The man at her elbow talks on. She does not hear. She is still looking—a little swifter, a little more anxiously—her red lips ready to droop in disappointment.

The noise of feet, of falling seats, continues. Boys call shrilly. Ushers dart hastily to and fro. The soft laughter and hum of talk come up from below.

She has reached the second balcony. She sweeps it hurriedly. Her companion raises his eyes to the same balcony and laughs as he speaks. She colors a little, but smiles as she lifts her eyes to the third balcony.

Suddenly the glass stops. The color surges up her neck, splashing her cheeks with red. Her breath stops also for a moment, then returns quick and strong.

Her smile settles into a curious contraction that is almost painful to see. His unsmiling eyes are looking somberly, sternly, accusingly into hers. They are charged with all the bitterness and hate and disappointed ambition which social injustice and inequality had wrought into his soul.

She shivered and dropped her glass. Shivered and drew her fleecy, pink and pale-blue cloak closer about her bare neck.

Her face grew timid, almost appealing, as she turned it upward toward him like a flower, to be kissed across the height that divided him from her.

Hamlin Garland

His heart swelled with exultation. His face softened. From the height of his intellectual pride he bent his head and sent a winged caress fluttering down upon that flowerlike face.

And then the stealing harmony of the violins began, gliding like mist above the shuddering, tumultuous, obscure thunder of the drums, and the man's soul swept across that sea of song with the heart of a lion and the wings of an eagle.

A tender, musing smile was on the woman's lips.

A PREACHER'S LOVE STORY

I

The train drew out of the great Van Buren Street depot at 4.30 of a dark day in late October. A tall young man, with a timid look in his eyes, was almost the last one to get on, and his pale face wore a worried look as he dropped into an empty seat and peered out at the squalid buildings reeling past in the mist.

The buildings grew smaller, and vacant lots appeared stretching away in flat spaces, broken here and there by ridges of ugly squat little tenement blocks. Over this landscape vast banners of smoke streamed, magnified by the misty rain which was driven in from the lake.

At last there came a swell of land clothed on with trees. It was still light enough to see they were burr oaks, and the young student's heart thrilled at sight of them. His forehead smoothed out, and his eyes grew tender with boyish memories.

He was seated thus, with head leaning against the pane, when another young man came down the aisle from the smoking car and took a seat beside him with a pleasant word.

He was a handsome young fellow of twenty-three or four. His face was large and beardless, and he had beautiful teeth. He had a bold and keen look, in spite of the bang of yellow hair which hung over his forehead.

Some commonplaces passed between them, and then silence fell on each. The conductor coming through the car, the smooth-faced young fellow put up a card to be punched, and the student handed up a ticket, simply saying, "Kesota."

After a decent pause the younger man said "Going to Kesota, are you?"

"Yes."

"So am I. I live there, in fact."

"Do you? Then perhaps you can tell me the name of your County Superintendent. I'm looking for a school." He smiled frankly. "I'm just out of Jackson University, and—"

"That so? I'm an Ann Arbor man myself." They took a moment for mutual warming up. "Yes, I know the Superintendent. Why not come right up to my boarding place, and to-morrow I'll introduce you? Looking for a school, eh? What kind of a school?"

"Oh, a village school, or even a country school. It's too late to get a good place; but I've been sick, and—"

"Yes, the good positions are all snapped up; still, you might by accident hit on something. I know Mott; he'll do all he can for you. By the way, my name's Allen."

The young student understood this hint and spoke. "Mine is Stacey."

The younger man mused a few minutes, as if he had forgotten his new acquaintance. Suddenly he roused up.

"Say, would you take a country school several miles out?"

"I think I would, if nothing better offered."

"Well, out in my neighborhood they're without a teacher. It's six miles out, and it isn't a lovely neighborhood. However, they will pay fifty dollars a month; that's ten dollars extra for the scrimmages. They wanted me to teach this winter—my sister teaches it in summer—but, great Peter! I can't waste my time teaching school, when I can run up to Chicago and take a shy at the pit and make a whole term's wages in thirty minutes."

"I don't understand," said Stacey.

"Wheat Exchange. I've got a lot of friends in the pit, and I can come in any time on a little deal. I'm no Jim Keene, but I hope to get cash enough to handle five thousand. I wanted the old gent to start me up in it, but he said, 'Nix come arouse.' Fact is, I dropped the money he gave me to go through college with." He smiled at Stacey's disapproving look. "Yes, indeedy; there's where the jar came into our tender relations. Oh, I call on the governor—always when I've got a wad. I have fun with him." He smiled brightly. "Ask him if he don't need a little cash to pay for hog-killin', or something like that." He laughed again. "No, I didn't graduate at Ann Arbor. Funny how things go, ain't it? I was on my way back the third year, when I stopped in to see the pit—it's one o' the sights of Chicago, you know—and Billy Krans saw me looking over the rail. I went in, won, and then took a flyer on December. Come a big slump, and I failed to materialize at school."

Hamlin Garland

"What did you do then?" asked Stacey, to whom this did not seem humorous.

"I wrote a contrite letter to the governor, stating case, requesting forgiveness—and money. No go! Couldn't raise neither. I then wrote casting him off. 'You are no longer father of mine.'" He smiled again radiantly. "You should have seen me the next time I went home! Plug hat! Imported suit! Gold watch! Diamond shirt-stud! Cost me $200 to paralyze the general, but I did it. My glory absolutely turned him white as a sheet. I knew what he thought, so I said: 'Perfectly legitimate, dad. The walls of Joliet are not gaping for me.' That about half fetched him—calling him *dad*, I mean—but he can't get reconciled to my business. 'Too many ups and downs,' he says. Fact is, he thinks it's gambling, and I don't argue the case with him. I'm on my way home now to stay over Sunday."

The train whistled, and Allen looked out into the darkness. "We're coming to the crossing. Now, I can't go up to the boarding place when you do, but I'll give you directions, and you tell the landlady I sent you, and it'll be all right. Allen, you remember—Herman Allen."

Following directions, Stacey came at length to a two-story frame house situated on the edge of the bank, with its back to the river. It stood alone, with vacant lots all about. A pleasant-faced woman answered the ring.

He explained briefly. "How do you do? I'm a teacher, and I'd like to get board here a few days while passing my examinations. Mr. Herman Allen sent me."

The woman's quick eye and ear were satisfied. "All right. Walk in, sir. I'm pretty full, but I expect I can accommodate you—if you don't mind Mr. Allen for a roommate."

"Oh, not at all," he said, while taking off his coat.

"Come right in this way. Supper will be ready soon."

He went into a comfortable sitting room, where a huge open fire of soft coal was blazing magnificently. The walls were papered in florid patterns, and several enlarged portraits were on the walls. The fire was the really great adornment; all else was cheap, and some of it was tawdry.

Stacey spread his thin hands to the blaze, while the landlady sat down a moment, out of politeness, to chat, scanning him keenly. She was a handsome woman, strong, well rounded, about forty years of age, with quick gray eyes and a clean, firm-lipped mouth.

"Did you just get in?"

"Yes. I've been on the road all day," he said, on an impulse of communication. "Indeed, I'm just out of college."

"Is that so?" exclaimed Mrs. Mills, stopping her rocking in an access of interest. "What college?"

"Jackson University. I've been sick, and only came West—"

There came a look into her face that transformed and transfigured her. "*My* boy was in Ann Arbor. He was killed on the train on his way home one day." She stopped, for fear of breaking into a quaver, and smiled brightly. "That's why I always like college boys. They all stop here with me." She rose hastily. "Well, you'll excuse me, won't you, and I'll go an' 'tend to supper."

There was a great deal that was feminine in Stacey, and he felt at once the pathos of the woman's life. He looked a refined, studious, rather delicate young man, as he sat low in his chair and observed the light and heat of the fire. His large head looked to be full of learning, and his dark eyes were deep with religious fervor.

Several young women entered, and the room was filled with clatter of tongues. Herman came in a few moments later, his face in a girlish glow of color. Everybody rushed at him with loud outcry. He was evidently a great favorite. He threw his arms about Mrs. Mills, giving her a hearty hug. The girls pretended to be shocked when he reached out for them, but they were not afraid of him. They hung on his arms and besieged him with questions till he cried out, in jolly perplexity:

"Girls, girls! This will never do."

Mrs. Mills brushed out his damp yellow curls with her hands. "You're all wet."

"Girls, if you'll let me sit down, I'll take one on each knee," he said, pleadingly, and they released him.

Stacey grew red with sympathetic embarrassment, and shrank away into a corner.

"Go get supper ready," commanded Herman. And it was only after they left that he said to Stacey: "Oh, you found your way all right. I didn't see you—those confounded girls bother me so." He took a seat by the fire and surveyed his wet shoes. "I took a run up to Mott's house—only a half block out o' the way. He said they'd be tickled to have you at Cyene. By the way, you're a theolog, aren't you?" Wallace nodded, and Herman went on: "So I told Mott. He said you might work up a society out there at Cyene."

"Is there a church there?"

"Used to be, but—say, I tell you what you do: you go out with me to-morrow, and I'll give you the whole history."

The ringing of the bell took them out into the cheerful dining room in a good-natured scramble. Mrs. Mills put Stacey at one end of the table, near a young woman who looked like a teacher, and he had full sweep of the table, which was surrounded by bright and sunny faces. The station hand was there, and a couple of grocery clerks, and a brakeman sat at Stacey's right hand. The table was very merry. They called each other by their Christian names, and there was very obvious courtship on the part of several young couples.

Stacey escaped from the table as soon as possible, and returned to his seat beside the fire. He was young enough to enjoy the chatter of the girls, but his timidity made him glad they paid so little attention to him. The rain had changed to sleet outside, and hammered at the window viciously, but the blazing fire and the romping young people set it at defiance. The landlady came to the door of the dining room, dish and cloth in hand, to share in each outburst of laughter, and not infrequently the hired girl peered over her shoulder with a broad smile on her face. A little later, having finished their work, they both came in and took active part in the light-hearted fun.

Herman and one of the girls were having a great struggle over some trifle he had snatched from her hand, and the rest stood about laughing to see her desperate attempts to recover it. This was a familiar form of courtship in Kesota, and an evening filled with such romping was considered a "cracking good time." After the girl, red and disheveled, had given up, Herman sat down at the organ, and they all sang Moody and Sankey hymns, negro melodies, and college songs till nine o'clock. Then Mrs. Mills called, "Come, now, boys and girls," and they all said good night, like obedient children.

Herman and Wallace went up to their bedroom together.

"Say, Stacey, have you got a policy?" Wallace shook his head. "And don't want any, I suppose. Well, I just asked you as a matter of form. You see," he went on, winking at Wallace comically, "nominally I'm an insurance agent, but practically I'm a 'lamb'—but I get a mouthful o' fur myself occasionally. What I'm working for is to get on that Wheat Exchange. That's where you get life! I'd rather be an established broker in that howling mob than go to Congress."

Suddenly a thought struck him. He rose on his elbow in bed and looked at Wallace just as he rose from a silent prayer. Catching his eye, Herman said:

"Say! why didn't you shout? I forgot all about it—I mean your profession."

Wallace crept into bed beside his communicative bedfellow in silence. He didn't know how to deal with such spirits.

"Say!" called Herman suddenly, as they were about to go to sleep, "you ain't got no picnic, old man."

"Why, what do you mean?"

"Wait till you see Cyene Church. Oh, it's a daisy snarl."

"I wish you'd tell me about it."

"Oh, it's quiet now. The calmness of death," said Herman. "Well, you see, it came this way. The church is made up of Baptists and Methodists, and the Methodists wanted an organ, because, you understand, father was the head center, and Mattie is the only girl among the Methodists who can play. The old man has got a head like a mule. He can't be switched off, once he makes up his mind. Deacon Marsden he don't believe in anything above tuning forks, and he's tighter'n the bark on a bulldog. He stood out like a sore thumb, and dad wouldn't give an inch.

"You see, they held meetings every other Sunday. So dad worked up the organ business and got one, and then locked it up when the Baptists held their services. Well, it went from bad to worse. They didn't speak as they passed by—that is, the old folks; we young folks didn't care a continental whether school kept or not. Well, upshot is, the church died out. The wind blew the horse sheds down, and there they lie—and the church is standing there empty as an—old boot —and—" He grew too sleepy to finish.

Suddenly a comical idea roused him again. "Say, Stacey—by Jinks!—are you a Baptist?"

"Yes."

"Oh, Peter! ain't that lovely?" He chuckled shamelessly, and went off to sleep without another word.

II

Herman was still sleeping when Stacey rose and dressed and went down to breakfast. Mrs. Mills defended Herman against the charge of laziness: "He's probably been out late all the week."

Stacey found Mott in the county courthouse, and a perfunctory examination soon put him in possession of a certificate. There was no question of his attainments.

Herman met him at dinner-time.

"Well, elder, I'm going down to get a rig to go out home in. It's colder'n a blue whetstone, so put on all the clothes you've got. Gimme your check, and I'll get your traps. Have you seen Mott?"

"Yes."

"Well, then, everything's all fixed."

He turned up about three o'clock, seated on the spring seat of a lumber wagon beside a woman, who drove the powerful team. Whether she was young or old could not be told through her wraps. She wore a cap and a thick, faded cloak.

Mrs. Mills hurried to the door. "Why, Mattie Allen! What you doin' out such a day as this? Come in here instanter!"

"Can't stop," called a clear, boyish voice. "Too late."

"Well, land o' stars!—you'll freeze."

When Wallace reached the wagon side, Herman said, "My

sister, Stacey."

The girl slipped her strong brown hand out of her huge glove and gave him a friendly grip. "Get right in," she said. "Herman, you're going to stand up behind."

Herman appealed to Mrs. Mills for sympathy. "This is what comes of having plebeian connections."

"Oh, dry up," laughed the girl, "or I'll make you drive."

Stacey scrambled in awkwardly beside her. She was not at all embarrassed, apparently.

"Tuck yourself in tight. It's mighty cold on the prairie."

"Why didn't you come down with the baroosh?" grumbled Herman.

"Well, the corn was contracted for, and father wasn't able to come—he had another attack of neuralgia last night after he got the corn loaded—so I had to come."

"Sha'n't I drive for you?" asked Wallace.

"No, thank you. You'll have all you can do to keep from freezing." She looked at his thin coat and worn gloves with keen eyes. He could see only her pink cheeks, strong nose, and dark, smiling eyes.

It was one of those terrible Illinois days when the temperature drops suddenly to zero, and the churned mud of the highways hardens into a sort of scoriac rock, which cripples the horses and sends the heavy wagons booming and thundering along like mad things. The wind was keen and terrible as a saw-bladed sword, and smote incessantly. The desolate sky was one thick, impenetrable mass of swiftly flying clouds. When they swung out upon the long pike leading due north, Wallace drew his breath with a gasp, and bent his head to the wind.

"Pretty strong, isn't it?" shouted Mattie.

"Oh, the farmer's life is the life for me, tra-la!" sang Herman, from his shelter behind the seat.

Mattie turned. "What do you think of *Penelope* this month?"

"She's a-gitten there," said Herman, pounding his shoe heels.

"She's too smart for young Corey. She ought to marry a man like Bromfield. My! wouldn't they talk?"

"Did y' get the second bundle of magazines last Saturday?"

"Yes; and dad found something in the *Popular Science* that made him mad, and he burned it."

"Did 'e? Tum-la-la! Oh, the farmer's life for me!"

"Are you cold?" she asked Wallace.

He turned a purple face upon her. "No—not much."

"I guess you better slip right down under the blankets," she advised.

The wind blew gray out of the north—a wild blast which stopped the young student's blood in his veins. He hated to give up, but he could no longer hold the blankets up over his knees, so he slipped down into the corner of the box, with his back to the wind, with the blankets drawn over his head.

The powerful girl slapped the reins down on the backs of the snorting horses, and encouraged them with shouts like a man: "Get out o' this, Dan! Hup there, Nellie!"

The wagon boomed and rattled. The floor of the box seemed beaten with a maul. The glimpses Wallace had of the land appalled him, it was so flat and gray and bare. The houses seemed poor, and drain-pipe scattered about told how wet it all was.

Herman sang at the top of his voice, and danced, and pounded his feet against the wagon box. "This ends it! If I can't come home without freezing to death, I don't come. I should have hired a rig, irrespective of you—"

The girl laughed. "Oh, you're getting thin-blooded, Herman. Life in the city has taken the starch all out of you."

"Better grow limp in a great city than freeze stiff in the country," he replied.

An hour's ride brought them into a yard before a large gray-white frame house.

Herman sprang out to meet a tall old man with head muffled up. "Hello, dad! Take the team. We're just naturally froze solid—at least I am. This is Mr. Stacey, the new teacher."

"How de do? Run in; I'll take the horses."

Herman and Wallace stumbled toward the house, stiff and bent.

Herman flung his arms about a tall woman in the kitchen door. "Hello, muz!" he said. "This is Mr. Stacey, the new teacher."

"Draw up to the fire, sir. Herman, take his hat and coat."

Mattie came in soon with a boyish rush. She was gleeful as a happy babe. She unwound the scarf from her head and neck, and hung up her cap and cloak like a man, but she gave her hair a little touch of feminine care, and came forward with both palms pressed to her burning cheeks.

"Did you suffer, child?" asked Mrs. Allen.

"No; I enjoyed it."

Herman looked at Stacey. "I believe on my life she did."

"Oh, it's fun. I don't get a chance to do anything so exciting very often."

Herman clicked his tongue. "Exciting? Well, well!"

"You must remember things are slower here," Mattie explained.

She came to light much younger than Stacey thought her. She was not eighteen, but her supple and splendid figure was fully matured. Her hair hung down her back in a braid, which gave a subtle touch of childishness to her.

"Sis, you're still a-growin'," Herman said, as he put his arm around her waist and looked up at her.

She seemed to realize for the first time that Stacey was a young man, and her eyes fell.

"Well, now, set up the chairs, child," said Mrs. Allen.

When the young teacher returned from his cold spare room

off the parlor the family sat waiting for him. They all drew up noisily, and Allen said:

"Ask the blessing, sir?"

Wallace said grace.

As Allen passed the potatoes he continued:

"My son tells me you are a minister of the gospel."

"I have studied for it."

"What denomination?"

"Tut, tut!" warned Herman. "Don't start any theological rabbits to-night, dad. With jaw swelled up you won't be able to hold your own."

"I'm a Baptist," Stacey answered.

The old man's face grew grim. It had been ludicrous before with its swollen jaw. "Baptist?" The old man turned to his son, whose smile angered him. "Didn't you know no more'n to bring a Baptist preacher into this house?"

"There, there, father!" began the wife.

"Be quiet. I'm boss of this shanty."

Herman struck in: "Don't make a show of yourself, old man. Don't mind the old gent, Stacey; he's mumpy to-day, anyhow."

Stacey rose. "I guess I—I'd better not stay—I—"

"Oh, no, no! Sit down, Stacey. It's all right. The old man's a little acid at me. He doesn't mean it."

Stacey got his coat and hat. His heart was swollen with indignation. He felt as if something fine were lost to him, and the cold outside was so desolate now.

Mrs. Allen was in tears; but the old man, having taken his stand, was going to keep it.

Herman lost his temper a little. "Well, dad, you're a little the cussedest Christian I ever knew. Stacey, sit down. Don't you be a fool just because he is—"

Stacey was buttoning his coat with trembling hands, when Martha went up to him.

"Don't go," she said. "Father's sick and cross. He'll be sorry for this to-morrow."

Wallace looked into her frank, kindly eyes and hesitated.

Herman said: "Dad, you are a lovely follower of Christ. You'll apologize for this, or I'll never set foot on your threshold again."

Stacey still hesitated. He was hurt and angry, but being naturally a sweet and gentle nature, he grew sad, and, yielding to the pressure of the girl's hand on his arm, he began to unbutton his overcoat.

She helped him off with it, and hung it back on the nail. She did not show tears, but her face was unwontedly grave.

They sat at the table again, and Herman and Mattie tried to restore something of the brightness which had been lost.

Allen sat grimly eating, his chin pushed down like a hog's snout.

After supper, as his father was about retiring to his bedroom, Herman fixed his bright eyes on him, and something very hard and masterful came into his boyish face.

"Old man—you and I haven't had a settlement on this thing yet. I'll see you later."

Allen shrank before his son's look, but shuffled sullenly off without uttering a word.

Herman turned to Wallace. "Stacey, I want to beg your pardon for getting you into this scrape. I didn't suppose the old gentleman would act like that. The older he gets, the more his New Hampshire granite shows. I hope you won't lay it up against me."

Wallace was too conscientious to say he didn't mind it, but he took Herman's hand in a quick clasp.

"Let's have a song," proposed Herman. "Music hath charms to soothe the savage breast, to charm a rock, and split a cabbage."

They went into the best room, where a fire was blazing, and Mattie and Herman sang hymns and old-fashioned love songs and college glees wonderfully intermingled. They ended by singing "Lorena," a wailing, supersentimental love song current in war times, and when they looked around there was a lofty look on the face of the young preacher—a look of exaltation, of consecration and resolve.

III

The next morning, at breakfast, Herman said, as he seized a hot biscuit, "We'll dispense with grace this morning, and till after the war is over." But Wallace blessed his bread in a silent prayer, and Mattie thought it very brave of him to do so.

Herman was full of mockery. "The sun rises just the same, whether it's 'sprinkling' or 'immersion.' It's lucky Nature don't take a hand in these theological contests—she doesn't even referee the scrap. She never seems to care whether you are sparring for points or fighting to a finish. What you theologic middle-weights are really fighting for I can't see—and I don't care, till you fall over the ropes on to my corns."

Stacey listened in a daze to Herman's tirade. He knew it was addressed to Allen, and that it deprecated war, and that it was mocking. The fresh face and smiling lips of the young girl seemed to put Herman's voice very far away. It was such a beautiful thing to sit at table with a lovely girl.

After breakfast he put on his cap and coat and went out into the clear, cold November air. All about him the prairie extended, marked with farmhouses and lined with leafless hedges. Artificial groves surrounded each homestead, relieving the desolateness of the fields.

Down the road he saw the spire of a small white church, and he walked briskly toward it, Herman's description in his mind.

As he came near he saw the ruined sheds, the rotting porch, and the windows boarded up, and his face grew sad. He tried one of the doors, and found it open. Some tramp had broken the lock. The inside was even more desolate than the outside.

It was littered with rotting straw and plum stones and melon seeds. Obscene words were scrawled on the walls, and even on the pulpit itself.

Taken altogether it was an appalling picture to the young servant of the Man of Galilee, a blunt reminder of the ferocity and depravity of man.

As he pondered the fire burned, and there rose again the flame of his resolution. He lifted his face and prayed that he might be the one to bring these people into the living union of the Church of Christ.

His blood set toward his heart with tremulous action. His eyes glowed with zeal like that of the Middle Ages. He saw the people united once more in this desecrated hall. He heard the bells ringing, the sound of song, the smile of peaceful old faces, and voices of love and fellowship filling the anterooms where hate now scrawled hideous blasphemy against woman and against God.

As he sat there Herman came in, his keen eyes seeking out every stain and evidence of vandalism.

"Cheerful prospect—isn't it?"

Wallace looked up with the blaze of his resolution still in his eyes. His pale face was sweet and solemn.

"Oh, how these people need Christ!"

Herman turned away. "They need killing—about two dozen of 'em. I'd like to have the job of indicating which ones; I wouldn't miss the old man, you bet!" he said, with blasphemous audacity.

Wallace was helpless in the face of such reckless thought, and so sat looking at the handsome young fellow as he walked about.

"Well, now, Stacey, I guess you'll need to move. I had another session with the old man, but he won't give in, so I'm off for Chicago. Mother's brother, George Chapman, who lives about as near the schoolhouse on the other side, will take you in. I guess we'd better go right down now and see about it. I've said good-by to the old man—for good this time; we didn't shake hands either," he said, as they walked down the road together. He was very stern and hard. Something of the father was hidden under his laughing exterior.

Stacey regretted deeply the necessity which drove him out of Allen's house. Mrs. Allen and Mattie had appealed to him very strongly. For years he had lived far from young women, and there was a magical power in the intimate home actions of this young girl. Her bare head, with simple arrangement of hair, someway seemed the most beautiful thing he had ever seen.

He thought of her as he sat at the table with George and his aged mother. They lived alone, and their lives were curiously silent. Once in a while a low-voiced question, and that was all.

George read the *Popular Science, Harper's Monthly Magazine*, and the *Open Court*, and brooded over them with slow intellectual movement. It was wonderful the amount of information he secreted from these periodicals. He was better informed than many college graduates.

He had little curiosity about the young stranger. He understood he was to teach the school, and he did not go further in inquiry.

He tried Wallace once or twice on the latest discoveries of John Fiske and Edison, and then gave him up and retired to his seat beside the sitting-room stove.

On the following Monday morning school began, and as Wallace took his way down the lane the wrecked church came again to his eyes. He walked past it with slow feet. His was a deeply religious nature, one that sorrowed easily over sin. Suffering of the poor did not trouble him; hunger seemed a little thing beside losing one's everlasting soul. Therefore to come from his studies upon such a monument of human depravity as this rotting church was to receive a shock and to hear a call to action.

Approaching the schoolhouse, his thought took a turn toward the scholars and toward Mattie. He had forgotten to ask her if she intended to be one of his pupils.

There were several children already gathered at the schoolhouse door as he came up. It was all very American—the boxlike house of white, the slender teacher approaching, the roughly clad urchins waiting.

He said, "Good morning, scholars."

They chorused a queer croak in reply—hesitating, inarticulate, shy. He unlocked the door and entered the cold, bare room—familiar, unlovely, with a certain power of primitive associations. In such a room he had studied his primer and his Ray's Arithmetic. In such a room he had made gradual recession from the smallest front seat to the back wall seat; and from one side of such a room to the other he had furtively worshiped a graceful girlish head.

He allowed himself but a moment of such dreaming, and then he assumed command, and with his ready helpers a fire

Hamlin Garland

was soon started. Other children came in, timorous as rabbits, slipping by with one eye fixed on him like scared chickens. They pre-empted their seats by putting down books and slates, and there arose sly wars for possession, which he felt in curious amusement—it was so like his own life at that age.

He assumed command as nearly in the manner of the old-time teachers as he could recall, and the work of his teaching was begun. The day passed quickly, and as he walked homeward again there stood that rotting church, and in his mind there rose a surging emotion larger than he could himself comprehend—a desire to rebuild it by uniting the warring factions, of whose lack of Christianity it was fatal witness.

IV

Now this mystical thing happened. As this son of a line of preachers brooded on this unlovely strife among men, he lost the equipoise of the scholar and student of modern history. He grew narrower and more intense. The burden of his responsibility as a preacher of Christ grew daily more insupportable.

Toward the end of the week he announced preaching in the schoolhouse on Sunday afternoon, and at the hour set he found the room crowded with people of all ages and sorts.

His heart grew heavy as he looked out over the room on women nursing querulous children, on the grizzled faces of grim-looking men, who studied him with keen, unsympathetic eyes. He had hard, unfriendly material to work with. There were but few of the opposite camp present, while the Baptist leaders were all there, with more curiosity than sympathy in their faces.

They exulted to think the next preacher to come among them as an evangelist should be a Baptist.

After the singing, which would have dribbled away into failure but for Mattie, Wallace rose, looking very white and weak, and began his prayer. Some of the boys laughed when his voice stuck in his throat, but he went on to the end of an earnest supplication, feeling he had not touched them at all.

While they sang again, he sat looking down at them with dry throat and staring eyes. They seemed so hard, so unchristianlike. What could he say to them? He saw Mattie looking at him, and on the front seat sat three beautiful little girls huddled together with hands clasped; they were inexpressibly dainty by contrast. As he looked at them the thought came to him, What is the goodness of a girl—of a child? It is not partisan—it is not of creeds, of articles—it is goodness of thought, of deeds. His face lighted up with the inward feeling of this idea, and he rose resolutely.

"Friends, with the help of Christ I am come among you to do you good. I shall hold meetings each night here in the schoolhouse until we can unite and rebuild the church again. Let me say now, friends, that I was educated a Baptist. My father was a faithful worker in the Baptist Church, and so was his father before him. I was educated in a Baptist college, and I came here hoping to build up a Baptist Church." He paused.

"But I see my mistake. I am here to build up a Church of Christ, of good deeds and charity and peace, and so I here say I am no longer a Baptist or Methodist. I am only a preacher, and I will not rest until I rebuild the church which stands rotting away there." His voice rang with intellectual determination as he uttered those words.

The people listened. There was no movement now. Even the babies seemed to feel the need of being silent. When he began again it was to describe that hideous wreck. He delineated the falling plaster, the litter around the pulpit, the profanation of the walls. "It is a symbol of your sinful hearts," he cried.

Much more he said, carried out of himself by his passion. It was as if the repentant spirit of his denominational fathers were speaking through him; and yet he was not so impassioned that he did not see, or at least feel, the eyes of the strong young girl fixed upon him; his resolution he spoke looking at her, and a swift response seemed to leap from her eyes.

When it was over, some of the Methodists and one of the Baptists came up to shake hands with him, awkwardly wordless, and the pressure of their hands helped him. Many of the Baptist brethren slipped outside to discuss the matter. Some were indignant, others much more moved.

Allen went by him with an audible grunt of derision, and there was a dark scowl on his face, but Mattie smiled at him, with tears still in her eyes. She had been touched by his vibrant voice; she had no sins to repent of.

The skeptics of the neighborhood were quite generally sympathetic. "You've struck the right trail now, parson," said Chapman, as they walked homeward together. "The days of the old-time denominationalism are about played out."

But the young preacher was not so sure of it—now that his inspiration was gone. He remembered his debt to his college, to his father, to the denomination, and it was not easy to set aside the grip of such memories.

He sat late revolving the whole situation in his mind. When he went to bed it was still with him, and involved itself with his dreams; but always the young girl smiled upon him with sympathetic eyes and told him to go on—or so it seemed to him.

He was silent at breakfast. He went to school with a feeling that a return to teaching little tow-heads to count and spell was now impossible. He sat in his scarred and dingy desk, while they took their places, and his eyes had a passionate intensity of prayer in them which awed the pupils. He had assumed new grandeur and terror in their eyes. When they were seated he bowed his head and uttered a short plea for grace, and then he looked at them again.

On the low front seat, with dangling legs and red round faces, sat the little ones. Someway he could not call them to his knees and teach them to spell; he felt as if he ought to call them to him, as Christ did, to teach them love and reverence. It was impossible that they should not be touched by this hideous neighborhood of hate and strife.

Behind them sat the older children, some of them with rough, hard, sly faces. Some grinned rudely and nudged each other. The older girls sat with bated breath; they perceived something strange in the air. Most of them had heard his sermon the night before.

At last he broke silence. "Children, there is something I must say to you this morning. I'm going to have meeting here to-night, and it may be I shall not be your teacher any more—I mean in school. I wish you'd go home to-day and tell your people to come to church here to-night. I wish you'd all come yourselves. I want you to be good. I want you to love God and be good. I want you to go home and tell your people the teacher can't teach you here till he has taught the older people to be kind and generous. You may put your books away, and school will be dismissed."

The wondering children obeyed—some with glad promptness, others with sadness, for they had already come to like their teacher very much.

As he sat by the door and watched them file out, it was as if he were a king abdicating a throne, and these his faithful subjects. It was the most momentous hour of his life. He had set his face toward dark waters.

Mrs. Allen came over with Mattie to see him that day. She was a good woman, gentle and prayerful, and she said, with much emotion:

"O Mr. Stacey, I do hope you can patch things up here. If you could only touch his heart! He don't mean to do wrong, but he's so set in his ways—if he says a thing he sticks to it."

Stacey turned to Mattie for a word of encouragement, but she only looked away. It was impossible for her to put into words her feeling in the matter, which was more of admiration for his courage than for any part of his religious zeal. He was so different from other men. It seemed he had a touch of divinity in him now.

It did him good to have them come, and he repeated his vow:

"By the grace of our Lord, I am going to rebuild the Cyene Church," and his face paled and his eyes grew luminous.

The girl shivered with a sort of awe. He seemed to recede from her as he spoke, and to grow larger, too. Such nobility of purpose was new and splendid to her.

*   *   *   *   *

The revival was wondrously dramatic. The little schoolhouse was crowded to the doors night by night. The reek of stable-stained coats and boots, the smell of strong tobacco, the effluvia of many breaths, the heat, the closeness, were forgotten in the fervor of the young evangelist's utterances. His voice took on wild emotional cadences without his conscious effort, and these cadences sounded deep places in the heart. To these people, long unused to religious oratory, it was like the return of John and Isaiah. It was poetry and the drama, and processions and apocalyptic visions. He had the histrionic spell, too, and his slender body lifted and dilated, and his head took on majesty and power, and the fling of his white hand was a challenge and an appeal.

A series of stirring events took place on the third night.

On Wednesday Jacob Turner rose and asked the prayers of his neighbors, and was followed by two Baptist spearmen of the front rank. On Thursday the women all were weeping on each other's bosoms; only one or two of the men held out—old Deacon Allen and his antagonist, Stewart Marsden. Grim-visaged old figures they were, placed among repentant men and weeping women. They sat like rocks in the rush of the two factions moving toward each other for peaceful union. Granitic, narrow, keen of thrust, they seemed unmoved, while all around them one by one skeptics acknowledged the pathos and dignity of the preacher's views of life and death.

Meanwhile the young evangelist lived at high pressure. He grew thinner and whiter each night. He toiled in the daytime to formulate his thoughts for the evening. He could not sleep till far toward morning. The food he ate did him little good, while his heart went out constantly to his people in strenuous supplication. It was testimony of his human quality that he never for one moment lost that shining girl face out of his thought. He looked for it there night after night. It was his inspiration in speaking, as at the first.

On the nights when Mattie was not there his speech was labored (as the elders noticed), but on the blessed nights when she came and sang, her voice, amid all the rest, came to him, and uttered poetry and peace like a rill of cool sweet water. And afterward, when he walked home under the stars, his mind went with her, she was so strong and lithe and good to see. He did not realize the worshiping attitude the girl took before divine duties.

At last the great day came—the great night.

In some way, perhaps by the growing mass of rushing

emotion set in action by some deep-going phrase, or perhaps by some interior slow weakening of stubborn will, Deacon Allen gave way; and when the preacher called for penitents, the old man struggled to his feet, his seamed, weather-beaten face full of grotesque movement. He broke out:

"Brethren, pray for me; I'm a miserable sinner. I want to confess my sins—here—before ye all." He broke into sobbing terrible to hear. "My heart is made—flesh again—by the blessed power of Christ ..."

He struggled to get his voice. One or two cried, "Praise God!" but most of them sat silent, awed into immobility.

The old man walked up the aisle. "I've been rebellious—and now I want to shake hands with you all—and I ask your prayers." He bent down and thrust his hand to Marsden, his enemy, while the tears streamed down his face.

Marsden turned white with a sort of fear, but he rose awkwardly and grasped the outstretched hand, and at the touch of palms every soul rose as if by electric shock. "Amens!" burst forth. The preacher began a fervent prayer, and came down toward the grizzled, weeping old men, and they all embraced, while some old lady with sweet quavering voice raised a triumphal hymn, in which all joined, and found grateful relief from their emotional tension.

Allen turned to Mattie and his wife. "My boy—send for him—Herman."

It seemed as if the people could not go away. The dingy little schoolhouse was like unto the shining temple of God's grace, and the regenerated seemed to fear that to go home might become a return to hate and strife. So they clung around the young preacher and would not let him go.

At last he came out with Allen holding to his arm. "You must come home with us to-night," he pleaded, and the young minister with glad heart consented, for he hoped he might walk beside Mattie; but this was not possible. There were several others in the group, and they moved off two and two up the deep hollows which formed the road in the snow.

The young minister walked with head uplifted to the stars, hearing nothing of the low murmur of talk, conscious only of his great plans, his happy heart, and the strong young girl who walked before him.

In the warm kitchen into which they came he lost something of his spiritual tension, and became more humanly aware of the significance of sitting again with these people. He gave the girl his coat and hat, and then watched her slip off her knitted hood and her cloak. Her eyes shone with returning laughter, and her cheeks were flushed with blood.

Looking upon her, the young evangelist lost his look of exaltation, his eyes grew soft and his limbs relaxed. His silence was no longer rapt—it was the silence of delicious, drowsy reverie.

V

The next morning he did not rise at all. The collapse had come. The bad air, the nervous strain, the lack of sleep, had worn down his slender store of strength, and when the great victory came he fell like a tree whose trunk has been slowly gnawed across by teeth of silent saw. His drowse deepened into torpor.

In the bright winter morning, seated in a gay cutter behind a bay colt strung with slashing bells, Mattie drove to Kesota for the doctor. She felt the discord between the joyous jangle of the bells, the stream of sunlight, and the sparkle of snow crystals, but it only added to the poignancy of her anxiety.

She had not yet reached self-consciousness in her regard for the young preacher—she thought of him as a noble human being liable to death, and she chirped again and again to the flying colt, whose broad hoofs flung the snow in stinging showers against her face.

A call at the doctor's house set him jogging out along the lanes, while she sent a telegram to Herman. As she whirled bay Tom into the road to go home, her heart rose in relief that was almost exaltation. She loved horses. She always sang under her breath, chiming to the beat of their bells, when alone, and now she loosened the rein and hummed an old love song, while the powerful young horse squared away in a trot which was twelve miles an hour—*click,* click-*click,* click-*clangle,* lang-*lingle,* ling.

In such air, in such sun, who could die? Her good animal strength rose dominant over fear of death.

She came upon the doctor swinging along in his old blue

cutter, dozing in country-doctor style, making up for lost sleep.

"Out o' the way, doctor!" she gleefully called.

The doctor roused up and looked around with a smile. He was not beyond admiring such a girl as that. He snapped his whip-lash lightly on old Sofia's back, who looked up surprised, and, seeming to comprehend matters, began to reach out broad, flat, thin legs in a pace which the proud colt respected. She came of illustrious line, did Sofia, scant-haired and ungracious as she now was.

"Don't run over me," called the doctor, ironically, and with Sofia still leading they swung into the yard.

Mattie went in with the doctor, while Allen looked after both horses. They found Chapman attending Wallace—who lay in a dazed quiet—conscious, but not definitely aware of material things.

The doctor looked his patient over carefully. Then he asked, "Who is the yoong mon?"

"He's been teaching here, or rather preaching."

"When did this coom on?"

"Last night. Wound up a big revival last night, I believe. Kind o' caved in, I reckon."

"That's all. Needs rest. He'll be wearin' a wood jacket if he doosna leave off preachin'."

"Regular jamboree. I couldn't stop him. One of these periodical neighborhood 'awakenings,' they call it."

"They have need of it here, na doot."

"Well, they need something—love for God—or man."

"M—well! It's lettle I can do. The wumman can do more, if the mon'll be eatin' what they cuke for 'im," said the candid old Scotchman. "Mak' 'im eat. Mak' 'im eat."

Once more Tom pounded along the shining road to Kesota to meet the six-o'clock train from Chicago.

Herman, magnificently clothed in fur-lined ulster and cap, alighted with unusually grave face and hurried toward Mattie.

"Well, what is it, sis? Mother sick?"

"No; it's the teacher. He is unconscious. I've been for the doctor. Oh, we were scared!"

He looked relieved, but a little chagrined. "Oh, well, I don't see why I should be yanked out of my boots by a telegram because the teacher is sick! He isn't kin—yet."

For the first time a feeling of shame and confusion swept over Mattie, and her face flushed.

Herman's keen eyes half closed as he looked into her face.

"Mat—what—what! Now look here—how's this? Where's Ben Holly's claim?"

"He never had any." She shifted ground quickly. "O Herman, we had a wonderful time last night! Father and Uncle Marsden shook hands—"

"What?" shouted Herman, as he fell in a limp mass against the cutter. "Bring a physician—I'm stricken."

"Don't act so! Everybody's looking."

"They'd better look. I'm drowning while they wait."

She untied the horse and came back.

"Climb in there and stop your fooling, and I'll tell you all about it."

He crawled in with tearing groans of mock agony, and then leaned his head against her shoulder. "Well, go on, sis; I can bear it now."

She nudged him to make him sit up.

"Well, you know we've had a revival."

"So you wrote. Must have been a screamer to fetch dad and old Marsden. A regular Pentecost of Shinar."

"It was—I mean it was beautiful. I saw father was getting stirred up. He prayed almost all day yesterday, and at night —Well, I can't tell you, but Wallace talked, oh, so beautiful and tender."

"She calls him Wallace?" mused Herman, like a comedian.

"Hush! And then came the hand-shaking, and then the minister came home with us, because father asked him to."

"Well, well! I supposed *you* must have asked him."

The girl was hurt, and she showed it. "If you make fun, I

won't tell you another word," she said.

"Away Chicago! enter Cyene! Well, come, I won't fool any more."

"Then after Wallace—I mean—"

"Let it stand. Come to the murder."

"Then father came and asked me to send for you, and mother cried, and so did he. And, oh, Hermie, he's so sweet and kind! Don't make fun of him, will you? It's splendid to have him give in, and everybody feels glad that the district will be all friendly again."

Herman did not gibe again. His voice was gentle. The pathos in the scene appealed to him. "So the old man sent for me himself, did he?"

"Yes; he could hardly wait till morning. But this morning, when we came to call the teacher, he didn't answer, and father went in and found him unconscious. Then I went for the doctor."

Bay Tom whirled along in the splendid dusk, his nostrils flaring ghostly banners of steam on the cold crisp air. The stars overhead were points of green and blue and crimson light, low-hung, changing each moment.

Their influence entered the soul of the mocking young fellow. He felt very solemn, almost melancholy, for a moment.

"Well, sis, I've got something to tell you all. I'm going to tell it to you by degrees. I'm going to be married."

"Oh!" she gasped, with quick, indrawn breath. "Who?"

"Don't be ungrammatical, whatever you do. She's a cashier in a restaurant, and she's a fine girl," he added steadily, as if combating a prejudice. He forgot for the moment that such prejudices did not exist in Cyene.

Sis was instantly tender, and very, very serious.

"Of course she is, or you wouldn't care for her. Oh, I'd like to see her!"

"I'll take you up some day and show her to you."

"Oh, will you? Oh, when can I go?" She was smit into gravity again. "Not till the teacher is well."

Herman pretended to be angry. "Dog take the teacher, the old spindle-legs! If I'd known he was going to raise such a ruction in our quiet and peaceful neighborhood, I never would have brought him here."

Mattie did not laugh; she pondered. She never quite understood her brother when he went off on those queer tirades, which might be a joke or an insult. He had grown away from her in his city life.

They rode on in silence the rest of the way, except now and then an additional question from Mattie concerning his sweetheart.

As they neared the farmhouse she lost interest in all else but the condition of the young minister. They could see the light burning dimly in his room, and in the parlor and kitchen as well, and this unusual lighting stirred the careless young man deeply. It was associated in his mind with death and birth, and also with great joy.

The house was lighted so the night his elder brother died, and it looked so to him when he whirled into the yard with the doctor when Mattie was born.

"Oh, I hope he isn't worse!" said the girl, with deep feeling.

Herman put his arm about her, and she knew he knew.

"So do I, sis."

Allen came to the door as they drove in, and the careless boy realized suddenly the emotional tension his father was in. As the old man came to the sleigh-side he could not speak. His fingers trembled as he took the outstretched hand of his boy.

Herman's voice shook a little:

"Well, dad, Mattie says the war is over."

The old man tried to speak, but only coughed and then he blew his nose. At last he said, brokenly:

"Go right in; your mother's waitin'."

It was singularly dramatic to the youth. To come from the careless, superficial life of his city companions into contact with such primeval passions as these, made him feel like a spectator at some new and powerful and tragic play.

His mother fell upon his neck and cried, while Mattie stood by pale and anxious. Inside the parlor could be heard the mumble of men's voices.

In such wise do death and the fear of death fall upon country homes. All day the house had swarmed with people. All day this mother had looked forward to the reconciliation of her husband with her son. All day had the pale and silent minister of God kept his corpselike calm, while all about the white snow gleamed, and radiant shadows filled every hollow, and the cattle bawled and frisked in the barnyard, and the fowls cackled joyously, while the mild soft wind breathed warmly over the land.

Mattie cried out to her mother in quick, low voice, "O mother, how is he?"

"He ain't no worse. The doctor says there ain't no immediate danger."

The girl brought her hands together girlishly, and said: "Oh, I'm so glad. Is he awake?"

"No; he's asleep."

"Is the doctor still here?"

"Yes."

"I guess I'll step in," said Herman.

The doctor and George Chapman sat beside the hard-coal heater, talking in low voices. The old doctor was permitting himself the luxury of a story of pioneer life. He rose with automatic courtesy, and shook hands with Herman.

"How's the sick man getting on?"

"Vera well—vera well—consederin' the mon is a complete worn-out—that's all—naethin' more. Thes floom-a-didale bezniss of rantin' away on the fear o' the Laird for sax weeks wull have worn out the frame of a bool-dawg."

Herman and Chapman smiled. "I hope you'll tell him that."

"Na fear, yoong mon," said the grim old warrior. "Weel, now ai'll juist be takin' anither look at him."

Herman went in with the doctor, and stood looking on while the old man peered and felt about. He came out soon, and leaving a few directions with Herman and Chapman, took his departure. Everything seemed favorable, he said.

There was no longer poignancy of anxiety in Mattie's mind, she was too much of a child to imagine the horror of loss, but she was grave and gay by turns. Her healthy and wholesome nature continually reasserted itself over the power of her newly attained woman's interest in the young preacher. She went to bed and slept dreamlessly, while Herman yawned and inwardly raged at the fix in which circumstances had placed him.

Like many another lover, days away from his sweetheart were lost days. He wondered how she would take all the life down here. It would be good fun to bring her down, anyway, and hear her talk. He planned such a trip, and grew so interested in the thought he forgot his patient.

In the early dawn Wallace rallied and woke. Herman heard the rustle of the pillow, and turned to find the sick man's eyes looking at him fixedly, calm but puzzled. Herman's lips slowly changed into a beautiful boyish smile, and Wallace replied by a faint parting of the lips, when Herman said:

"Hello, old man! How do you find yourself?" His hearty humorous greeting seemed to do the sick man good. Herman approached the bed. "Know where you are?" Wallace slowly put out a hand, and Herman took it. "You're coming on all right. Want some breakfast? Make it bucks?" he said, in Chicago restaurant slang. "White wings—sunny—one up coff."

All this was good tonic for Wallace, and an hour later he sipped broth, while Mrs. Allen and the Deacon and Herman stood watching the process with apparently consuming interest. Mattie was still soundly sleeping.

There began delicious days of convalescence, during which he looked peacefully out at the coming and going of the two women, each possessing powerful appeal to him—one the motherly presence which had been denied him for many years, the other something he had never permitted himself— a sweetheart's daily companionship.

He lay there planning his church, and also his home. Into the thought of a new church came shyly but persistently the thought of a fireside of his own, with this young girl sitting in the glow of it waiting for him. His life had held little romance in its whole length. He had earned his own way through school and to college. His slender physical energies had been taxed to their utmost at every stage of his climb, but now it seemed as though some blessed rest and peace were at hand.

Meanwhile, the bitter partisans met each other coming and going out of the gate of the Allen estate, and the goodness of God shone in their softened faces. Herman was skeptical of its lasting quality, but was forced to acknowledge that it was a lovely light. He it was who made the electrical suggestion to rebuild the church as an evidence of good faith. "You say you're regenerated—go ahead and regenerate the church," he said.

The enthusiasm of the neighborhood took flame. It should be done. A meeting was called. Everybody subscribed money or work. It was a generous outpouring of love and faith.

It was Herman also who counseled secrecy. "It would be a nice thing to surprise him," he said. "We'll agree to keep the scheme from him at home, if you don't give it away."

They set to work like bees. The women came down one day and took possession with brooms and mops and soap, and while the carpenters repaired the windows they fell savagely upon the grime of the seats and floors. The walls of the church echoed with woman's gossip and girlish laughter. Everything was scoured, from the door-hinges to the altar rails. New doors were hung and a new stove secured, and then came the painters to put a new coat of paint on the inside. The cold weather forbade repainting the outside.

The sheds were rebuilt by men whose hearts glowed with old-time fire. It was like pioneer days, when "barn-raising" and "bees" made life worth while in a wild, stern land. It was a beautiful time. The old men were moved to tears, and the younger rough men shouted cheery, boisterous cries to hide their own deep emotion. Hand met hand in heartiness never shown before. Neighbors frequented each other's homes, and the old times of visiting and brotherly love came back upon them. Nothing marred the perfect beauty of their revival— save the fear of its evanescence. It seemed too good to last.

Meanwhile love of another and merrier sort went on. The young men and maidens turned prayer meeting into trysts, and scrubbing bees into festivals. They rode from house to house under glittering stars, over sparkling snows, singing:

"Hallelujah! 'tis done:
I believe on the Son;

I am saved by the blood
Of the Crucified One."

And their rejoicing chorus was timed to the clash of bells on swift young horses. Who shall say they did not right? Did the Galilean forbid love and joy?

No matter. God's stars, the mysterious night, the bells, the watchful bay of dogs, the sting of snow, the croon of loving voices, the clasp of tender arms, the touch of parting lips— these things, these things outweigh death and hell, and all that makes the criminal tremble. Being saved, they must of surety rejoice.

And through it all Wallace crawled slowly back to life and strength. He ate of Mother Allen's chicken-broth and of toast from Mattie's care-taking hand, and gradually assumed color and heart. His solemn eyes looked at the powerful young girl with an intensity which seemed to take her strength from her. She would gladly have given her blood for him, if it had occurred to her, or if it had been suggested as a good thing; instead she gave him potatoes baked to a nicety, and buttered toast that would melt on the tongue, and, on the whole, they served the purpose better.

One day a smartly dressed man called to see Wallace. Mattie recognized him as the Baptist clergyman from Kesota. He came in, and introducing himself, said he had heard of the excellent work of Mr. Stacey, and that he would like to speak with him.

Wallace was sitting in a rocking chair in the parlor. Herman was in Chicago, and there was no one but Mrs. Allen and Mattie in the house.

The Kesota minister introduced himself to Wallace, and then

entered upon a long eulogium upon his work in Cyene. He asked after his credentials, his plans, his connections, and then he said:

"You've done a *fine* work in softening the hearts of these people. We had almost *despaired* of doing anything with them. Yes, you have done a *won-der-ful work*, and now we must reorganize a regular society here. I will be out again when you get stronger, and we'll see about it."

Wallace was too weak to take any stand in the talk, and so allowed him to get up and go away without protest or explanation of his own plans.

When Herman came down on Saturday, he told him of the Baptist minister's visit and the proposition. Herman stretched his legs out toward the fire and put his hands in his pockets. Then he rose and took a strange attitude, such as Wallace had seen in comic pictures—it was, in fact, the attitude of a Bowery tough.

"Say—look here! If you want 'o set dis community by de ears agin, you do dat ting—see? You play dat confidence game and dey'll rat ye—see? You invite us to come into a non-partisan deal—see?—and den you springs your own platform on us in de joint corkus—and we won't stand it! Dis goes troo de way it began, or we don't play—see?"

Out of all this Wallace deduced his own feeling—that continued peace and good-will lay in keeping clear of all doctrinal debates and disputes—the love of Christ, the desire to do good and to be clean. These emotions had been roused far more deeply than he realized, and he lifted his face to God in the hope that no lesser thing should come in to mar the beauty of his Church.

There came a day when he walked out in the sunshine, and heard the hens caw-cawing about the yard, and saw the young colts playing about the barn. And the splendor of the winter day dazzled him as if he were looking upon the broad-flung robe of the Most High. Everywhere the snow lay ridged with purple and brown hedges. Smoke rose peacefully from chimneys, and the sound of boys skating on a near-by pond added the human element.

The trouble of concealing the work of the community upon the church increased daily, and Mattie feared that some hint of it had come to him. She had her plan. She wanted to drive him down herself, and let him see the reburnished temple alone. But this was impossible. On the day when he seemed able to go, her father drove them all down. Marsden was there also, and several of his women-folks, putting down a new carpet on the platform. As they drew near the church, Wallace said:

"Why, they've fixed up the sheds!"

Mattie nodded. She was trembling with the delicious excitement of it—she wanted him hurried into the church at once. He had hardly time to think before he was whirled up to the new porch, and Marsden came out, followed by several women. He was bewildered by it all. Marsden helped him out with hearty voice sounding:

"Careful now. Don't hurry!"

Mattie took one arm, and so he entered the church. Everything repainted! Everything warm and bright and cozy!

The significance of it came to him like a wave of light, and he took his seat in the pulpit chair and stared at them all with a look on his pale face which moved them more than words.

He was like a man transfigured by an inward glow. His eyes for an instant flamed with this marvelous fire, then darkened, softened with tears, and his voice came back in a sob of joy, and he could only say:

"Friends—brethren!"

Marsden, after much coughing, said:

"We all united on this. We wanted to have you come to the church and—Well, we couldn't bear to have you see it again the way it was."

He understood it now. It was the sign of a united community. It set the seal of Christ's victory over evil passions, and the young preacher's head bowed in prayer, and they all knelt, while his weak voice returned thanks to the Lord for his gifts.

Then they all rose and shook off the oppressive solemnity, and he had time to look around at all the changes. At last he turned to Mattie and reached out his hand—he had the boldness of a man in the shadow of some mighty event which makes false modesty and conventions shadowy things of little importance. His sharpened interior sense read her clear soul, and he knew she was his, therefore he reached her his hand, and she came to him with a flush on her face, which died out as she stood proudly by his side, while he said:

"And Martha shall help me."

Therefore this good thing happened—that in the midst of his fervor and his consecration to God's work, the love of woman found a place.

A MEETING IN THE FOOTHILLS

I

The train which brought young Ramsey into Red Rock gave him no view of the mountains, because it arrived about eight o'clock of a dark day. He went to bed at once in order to be up early and prostrate himself before the peaks, for he was of the level middle-West.

He was awakened by the sound of loud, hearty voices, and looking out of the window saw a four-horse team standing before the little hotel. On the wagon's side was a sign which made the heart of the youth leap.

CRINKLE CREEK STAGE.
DAVE WILLIS, Pro.

He was in the land of gold! It was like a chapter from a story by Bret Harte. He dressed himself hurriedly, and went down and out into the cool, keen dawn, eager to catch a glimpse of the great peak whose name had been in his ear since a child, as the symbol of the Rocky Mountains.

There it soared, dull purple, splotched with dark green, and rising to white at its shoulders, and radiant with light on its crown. In such impassible grandeur, it must have loomed upon the eyes of the first little caravan trailing its way across the plains to the mysterious West.

He spent the day doing little else but gaze at the mountains and study the town.

It was also much more stupendous than he had imagined, and doubts of his ability to fit with all this splendor came to him with great force. He remembered the smooth, green swells and fertile fields he had left behind, and the memory brought a touch of homesickness.

After supper that evening he confided to the landlord his plans for finding a foreman's position on a stock farm.

"Well, I dunno. There are such places, but they're always snapped up 'fore you can say Jack Robinson."

"Well, I'm going to give it a good try," the young fellow said bravely.

"That's right. If I was you, I'd go out and see some of these real-estate fellers; they most always know what's going on."

"That's a good idea; much obliged. I'll tackle 'em to-morrow," said Arthur, and he went off to bed, feeling victory almost a tame bird in his hands.

The next forenoon he made his first attempt. He had determined on his speech, and he went into the first office with his song on his lips.

"I'm looking for a place on a dairy farm; I've had five years' practical experience, and am a graduate of the—Agricultural College. I'm after the position of bookkeeper and foreman."

The man looked at him gravely.

"You're aiming pretty high, young feller, for this country. There are plenty of chances to work, punching cattle, but I don't think chances are good for a foreman's place." He was a kindly man, and repented when he saw how the young man's face fell. "However, I'll give you some names of people to see."

On the whole, this was not so depressing, Arthur thought.

The next man made a mistake and took him for an investor. He rose with great cordiality.

"Ah, good morning, sir—good morning! Have a chair. Just in? Do you feel the draft there? Oh, all right!" Then he settled himself in his swivel chair and beamed his warmest. "Well, what do you think of our charming town?"

Arthur had not the heart to undeceive him, and so, saturated in agony sweat, crawled out at last, and went timidly on to the third man, who was kindly and interested in a way, and gave him the names of some ranchers likely to hire a hand. Some days passed in this sort of search and resulted in nothing materially valuable, but a strong quality came out in his nature. Defeat seemed to put a grim sort of resolution into his soul.

Following faint clews, Ramsey made long walks into the country, toiling from ranch to ranch over the dun-colored, lonely hills, dogged, persistent, with lips set grimly.

He was returning late one afternoon from one of these fruitless journeys. It was one of those strange days that come in all seasons at that altitude. The air was full of suspended mist—it did not rain, the road was almost dry under foot, and yet this all-pervasive moisture seemed soaking everything. It was, in fact, a cloud, for this whole land was a mountain top.

The road wound among shapeless buttes of red soil, the plain was clothed on its levels with a short, dry grass, and on the side of the buttes were scattering, scraggy cedars, looking at a distance like droves of cattle.

He sat down upon a little hummock to rest, for his feet ached with the long stretches of hilly road. The larks cried to him out of the mist, with their piercing sweet notes, cheerful and undaunted ever. There was a sudden lighting up of the day, as if the lark's song had shot the mist with silver light.

As he rose and started on with painful slowness, he heard the sound of horses' hoofs behind him, and a man in a yellow cart came swiftly out of the gray obscurity.

Arthur stepped aside to let him pass, but he could not help limping a little more markedly as the man looked at him. The man seemed to understand.

"Will you ride?" he asked.

Arthur glanced up at him and nodded without speaking. The stranger was a fine-looking man, with a military cut of beard, getting gray. His face was ruddy and smiling.

"Thank you. I am rather tired," Arthur said, as he settled into the seat. "I guess I'll have to own up, I'm about played out."

"I thought you looked foot-sore. I'm enough of a Western man to feel mean when I pass a man on the road. A footman can get very tired on these stretches of ours."

"I've tramped about forty miles to-day, I guess. I'm trying to

Hamlin Garland

find some work to do," he added, in desperate confidence.

"Is that so? What kind of work?"

"Well, I wanted to get a place as foreman on a ranch."

"I'm afraid that's too much to expect."

Arthur sighed.

"Yes, I suppose it is. If I'd known as much two weeks ago as I do now, I wouldn't be here."

"Oh, don't get discouraged; there's plenty of work to do. I can give you something to do on my place."

"Well, I've come to the conclusion that there is nothing here for me but the place of a common hand, so if you can give me anything—"

"Oh, yes, I can give you something to do in my garden. Perhaps something better will open up later. Where are you staying?" he asked, as they neared town.

Arthur told him, and the man drove him down to his hotel.

"I'd like to have you call at my office to-morrow morning; my partner does most of the hiring. I've been living in Denver. Here's my card."

After he had driven away, the listening landlord broke forth:

"You're in luck, Cap. If you get a place with Major Thayer you're fixed."

"Who is he, anyhow?"

"Who is he? Why, he owns all the land up the creek, and banks all over Colorado."

"Is that so?"

Arthur was delighted. Of course, it was only a common hand's place, but here was the vista he had looked for—here was the chance.

He stretched his legs under the table in huge content as he ate his supper. His youthful imagination had seized upon this slender wire of promise and was swiftly making it a hoop of diamonds.

II

When he entered the office next day, however, the Major merely nodded to him over the railing and said:

"Good morning. Take a seat, please."

He seemed deeply engaged with a tall young man of about thirty-five years of age, with a rugged, smooth-shaven face. The young man spoke with a marked English accent, and there was a quality in his manner of speech which appealed very strongly to Arthur.

"Confeound the fellow," the young Englishman was saying, "I've discharged him. I cawn't re-engage him, ye kneow! We cawn't have a man abeout who gets drunk, y' kneow—it's too bloody proveoking, Majah."

"But the poor fellow's family, Saulisbury."

"Oh, hang the fellow's family," laughed Saulisbury. "We are not a poorhouse, y' kneow—or a house for inebriates. I confess I deon't mind these things as you do, old man. I'm a Britisher, y' kneow, and I haven't got intristed in your bloody radicalism, y' kneow. I'm in for Sam Saulisbury 'from the word go,' as you fellows say."

"And you don't get along any better—I mean in a money way."

"I kneow, and that's too deuced queeah. Your blawsted sentimentality seems note to do you any harm. Still I put it in this way, y' kneow—if he weren't so deadly sentimental, what couldn't the fellow do, y' kneow?"

The Major laughed.

"Well, I can't turn Jackson off, even for you."

"Well, deon't do it then—only if he gets drunk agine and drops a match into the milk can, fancy! and blows us all up, deon't come back on me, that's all."

They both laughed at this, and the Major said:

"This is the young man I told you about, Mr.—a—"

"Ramsey is my name," said Arthur, rising.

"Mr. Ramsey, this is my partner, Mr. Saulisbury."

"Haow de do," said Saulisbury, with a nod and a glance, which made Arthur hot with wrath, coming as it did after the talk he had heard. Saulisbury did not take the trouble to rise. He merely swung round on his swivel chair and eyed the young stranger.

Arthur was not thick-skinned, and he had been struck for the first time by the lash of caste, and it raised a welt.

He choked with his rage and stood silent, while Saulisbury looked him over, and passed upon his good points, as if he were a horse. There was something in the lazy lift of his eyebrows which maddened Arthur.

"He looks a decent young fellow enough; I suppeose he'll do to try," Saulisbury said at last, with cool indifference. "I'll use him, Majah."

"By Heaven, you won't!" Arthur burst out. "I wouldn't work for you at any price."

He turned on his heel and rushed out.

He heard the Major calling to him as he went down the stairs, but refused to turn back. The tears of impotent rage filled his eyes, his fists strained together, and the curses pushed slowly from his lips. He wished he had leaped upon his insulter where he sat—the smooth, smiling hound!

He was dizzy with rage. For the first time in his life he had been trampled upon, and could not, at least he had not, struck his assailant.

As he stood on the street-corner thinking of these things and waiting for the mist of rage to pass from his eyes, he felt a hand on his arm, and turned to Major Thayer, standing by his side.

"Look here, Ramsey, you mustn't mind Sam. He's an infernal Englishman, and can't understand our way of meeting men. He didn't mean to hurt your feelings."

Arthur looked down at him silently, and there was a look in his eyes which went straight to the Major's heart.

"Come, Ramsey, I want to give you a place. Never mind this. You will really be working for me, anyhow."

Saulisbury himself came down the stairs and approached them, putting on his gloves, and Arthur perceived for the first time that his eyes were blue and very good-natured. Saulisbury cared nothing for the youth, but felt something was due his partner.

"I hope I haven't done anything unpardonable," he began, with his absurd, rising inflection.

Arthur flared up again.

"I wouldn't work for a man like you if I starved. I'm not a dog. You'll find an American citizen won't knuckle down to you the way your English peasants do. If you think you can come out here in the West and treat men like dogs, you'll find yourself mighty mistaken, that's all!"

The men exchanged glances. This volcanic outburst amazed Saulisbury, but the Major enjoyed it. It was excellent schooling for his English friend.

"Well, work for me, Mr. Ramsey. Sam knuckles down to me on most questions. I hope I know how to treat my men. I'm trying to live up to traditions, anyway."

"You'll admit it is a tradition," said Saulisbury, glad of a chance to sidle away.

The Major dismissed Saulisbury with a move of the hand.

"Now get into my cart, Mr. Ramsey, and we'll go out to the farm and look things over," he said; and Arthur clambered in.

"I can't blame you very much," the Major continued, after they were well settled. "I've been trying lately to get into harmonious relations with my employees, and I think I'm succeeding. I have a father and grandfather in shirt sleeves to start from and to refer back to, but Saulisbury hasn't. He means well, but he can't always hold himself in. He means to be democratic, but his blood betrays him."

Arthur soon lost the keen edge of his grievance under the kindly chat of the Major.

The farm lay on either side of a small stream which ran among the buttes and green mesas of the foothills. Out to the left, the kingly peak looked benignantly across the lesser heights that thrust their ambitious heads in the light. Cattle were feeding among the smooth, straw-colored or sage-green hills. A cluster of farm buildings stood against an abrupt, cedar-splotched bluff, out of which a stream flowed and shortly fell into a large basin.

The irrigation ditch pleased and interested Arthur, for it was the finest piece of work he had yet seen. It ran around the edge of the valley, discharging at its gates streams of water like veins, which meshed the land, whereon men were working among young plants.

"I'll put you in charge of a team, I think," the Major said, after talking with the foreman, a big, red-haired man, who looked at Arthur with his head thrown back and one eye shut.

"Well, now you're safe," said the Major, as he got into his buggy, "so I'll leave you. Richards will see you have a bed."

Arthur knew and liked the foreman's family at once. They were familiar types. At supper he told them of his plans, and how he came to be out there; and they came to feel a certain proprietorship in him at once.

"Well, I'm glad you've come," said Mrs. Richards, after their acquaintanceship had mellowed a day or two. "You're like our own folks back in Illinois, and I can't make these foreigners seem neighbors nohow. Not but what they're good enough, but, land sakes! they don't jibe in someway."

Arthur winced a little at being classed in with her folks, and changed the subject.

One Sunday, a couple of weeks later, just as he was putting on his old clothes to go out to do his evening's chores, the Major and a merry party of visitors came driving into the yard. Arthur came out to the carriage, a little annoyed that these city people should not have come when he had on his Sunday clothes. The Major greeted him pleasantly.

"Good evening, Ramsey. Just hitch the horses, will you? I want to show the ladies about a little."

Arthur tied the horses to a post and came back toward the Major, expecting him to introduce the ladies; but the Major did not, and Mrs. Thayer did not wait for an introduction, but said, with a peculiar, well-worn inflection:

"Ramsey, I wish you'd stand between me and the horses. I'm as afraid as death of horses and cows."

The rest laughed in musical uproar, but Arthur flushed hotly. It was the manner in which English people, in plays and stories, addressed their butler or coachman.

He helped her down, however, in sullen silence, for his rebellious heart seemed to fill his throat.

The party moved ahead in a cloud of laughter. The ladies were dainty as spring flowers in their light, outdoor dresses, and they seemed to light up the whole barnyard.

One of them made the most powerful impression upon Arthur. She was so dainty and so birdlike. Her dress was quaint, with puffed sleeves, and bands and edges of light green, like an April flower. Her narrow face was as swift as light in its volatile changes, and her little chin dipped occasionally into the fluff of her ruffled bodice like a swallow into the water. Every movement she made was strange and sweet to see.

She cried out in admiration of everything, and clapped her slender hands like a wondering child. Her elders laughed every time they looked at her, she was so entirely carried away by the wonders of the farm.

She admired the cows and the colts very much, but shivered prettily when the bull thrust his yellow and black muzzle through the little window of his cell.

"The horrid thing! Isn't he savage?"

"Not at all. He wants some meal, that's all," said the Major, as they moved on.

The young girl skipped and danced and shook her perfumed dress as a swallow her wings, without appearing vain—it was natural in her to do graceful things.

Arthur looked at her with deep admiration and delight, even while Mrs. Saulisbury was talking to him.

He liked Mrs. Saulisbury at once, though naturally prejudiced against her. She had evidently been a very handsome woman, but some concealed pain had made her face thin and drawn, and one corner of her mouth was set in a slight fold as if by a touch of paralysis. Her profile was still very beautiful, and her voice was that of a highly cultivated American.

She seemed to be interested in Arthur, and asked him a great many questions, and all her questions were intelligent.

Saulisbury amused himself by joking the dainty girl, whom he called Edith.

"This is the cow that gives the cream, ye know; and this one is the buttermilk cow," he said, as they stood looking in at the barn door.

Edith tipped her eager little face up at him:

"Really?"

The rest laughed again.

"Which is the ice-cream cow?" the young girl asked, to let them know that she was not to be fooled with.

Saulisbury appealed to the Major.

"Majah, what have you done with our ice-cream cow?"

"She went dry during the winter," said the Major; "no demand on her. 'Supply regulated by the demand,' you know."

They drifted on into the horse barn.

"We're in Ramsey's domain now," said the Major, looking at Arthur, who stood with his hand on the hip of one of the big gray horses.

Edith turned and perceived Arthur for the first time. A slight shock went through her sensitive nature, as if some faint prophecy of great storms came to her in the widening gaze of his dark eyes.

"Oh, do you drive the horses?" she asked quickly.

"Yes, for the present; I am the plowman," he said, in the wish to let her know he was not a common hand. "I hope to be promoted."

Her eyes rested a moment longer on his sturdy figure and his beautifully bronzed skin, then she turned to her companions.

After they had driven away, Arthur finished his work in silence; he could hardly bring himself to speak to the people at the supper table, his mind was in such tumult.

He went up into his little room, drew a chair to the window facing the glorious mountains, and sat there until the ingulfing gloom of rising night climbed to the glittering crown of white soaring a mile above the lights of the city; but he did not really see the mountains; his eyes only turned toward them as a cat faces the light of a hearth. It helped him to think, somehow.

He was naturally keen, sensitive, and impressionable; his mind worked quickly, for he had read a great deal and held his reading at command.

His thought concerned itself first of all with the attitude these people assumed toward him. It was perfectly evident that they regarded him as a creature of inferior sort. He was their servant.

It made him turn hot to think how terribly this contrasted with the flamboyant phraseology of his graduating oration. If the boys knew that he was a common hand on a ranch, and treated like a butler!

He came back for relief to the face of the girl, the girl who looked at him differently somehow.

The impression she made on him was one of daintiness and light; her eager face and her sweet voice, almost childish in its thin quality, appealed to him with singular force.

She was strange to him, in accent and life; she was good and sweet, he felt sure of that, but she seemed so far away in her manner of thought. He wished he had been dressed a little better; his old hat troubled him especially.

The girls he had known, even the daintiest of them, could drive horses and were not afraid of cows. Their way of talking was generally direct and candid, or had those familiar inflections which were comprehensible to him. She was alien.

Was she a girl? Sometimes she seemed a woman—when her face sobered a moment—then again she seemed a child. It was this change of expression that bewildered and fascinated him.

Then her lips were so scarlet and her level brown eyebrows wavered about so beautifully! Sometimes one had arched while the other remained quiet; this gave a winsome look of brightness and roguishness to her face.

He came at last to the strangest thing of all: she had looked at him, every time he spoke, as if she were surprised at finding herself able to understand his way of speech.

He worked it all out at last. They all looked upon him as belonging to the American peasantry; he belonged to a lower world—a world of service. He was brick, they were china.

Saulisbury and Mrs. Thayer were perfectly frank about it; they spoke from the English standpoint. The Major and Mrs. Saulisbury had been touched by the Western spirit and were trying to be just to him, with more or less unconscious patronization.

As his thoughts ran on, his fury came back, and he hammered

Hamlin Garland

and groaned and cursed as he tossed to and fro on his bed, determined to go back where the American ideas still held— back to the democracy of Lodi and Cresco.

III

These spring days were days of growth to the young man. He grew older and more thoughtful, and seldom joked with the other men.

There came to the surface moods which he had not known before. There came times when his teeth set together like the clutch of a wolf, as some elemental passion rose from the depths of his inherited self.

His father had been a rather morose man, jealous of his rights, quick to anger, but just in his impulses. Arthur had inherited these stronger traits, but they had been covered and concealed thus far by the smiling exterior of youth.

Edith came up nearly every day with the Major in order to enjoy the air and beauty of the sunshine, and when she did not come near enough to nod to Arthur, life was a weary treadmill for the rest of the day, and the mountains became mere gloomy stacks of *debris*.

Sometimes she sat on the porch with the children, while Mrs. Richards, the foreman's wife, a hearty, talkative woman, plied her with milk and cookies.

"It must be heaven to live here and feed the chickens and cows," the young girl said one day when Arthur was passing by—quite accidentally.

Mrs. Richards took a seat, wiping her face on her apron.

"Wal, I don't know about that, when it comes to waiting and tendin' on a mess of 'em; it don't edgicate a feller much. Does it, Art?"

"We don't do it for play, exactly," he replied, taking a seat on the porch steps and smiling up at Edith. "I can't stand cows; I like horses, though. Of course, if I were foreman of the dairy, that would be another thing."

The flowerlike girl looked down at him with a strange glance. Something rose in her heart which sobered her. She studied the clear brown of his face and the white of his forehead, where his hat shielded it from the sun and the wind. The spread of his strong neck, where it rose from his shoulders, and the clutch of his brown hands attracted her.

"How strong you look!" she said musingly.

He laughed up at her in frank delight.

"Well, I'm not out here for my health exactly, although when I came here I was pretty tender. I was just out of college, in fact," he said, glad of the chance to let her know that he was not an ignorant workingman.

She looked surprised and pleased.

"Oh, you're a college man! I have two brothers at Yale. One of them plays half-back or short-stop, or something. Of course you played?"

"Baseball? Yes, I was pitcher for '88." He heaved a sigh. He could not think of those blessed days without sorrow.

"Oh, I didn't mean baseball. I meant football."

"We don't play that much in the West. We go in more for baseball. More science."

"Oh, I like football best, it's so lively. I like to see them when they get all bunched up, they look so funny, and then when some fellow gets the ball under his arms and goes shooting around, with the rest all jumping at him. Oh, oh, it's exciting!"

She smiled, and her teeth shone from her scarlet lips with a more familiar expression than he had seen on her face before. Some wall of reserve had melted away, and they chatted on with growing freedom.

"Well, Edith, are you ready?" asked the Major, coming up.

Arthur sprang up as if he suddenly remembered that he was a workingman.

Edith rose also.

"Yes, all ready, uncle."

"Well, we'll be going in a minute.—Mr. Ramsey, do you think that millet has got water enough?"

"For the present, yes. The ground is not so dry as it looks."

As they talked on about the farm, Mrs. Richards brought out a glass of milk for the Major.

Arthur, with nice calculation, unhitched the horse and brought it around while the Major was detained.

"May I help you in, Miss Newell?"

She gave him her hand with a frank gesture, and the Major reached the cart just as she was taking the lines from Arthur.

"Are you coming?" she gayly cried. "If not, I'll drive home

by myself."

"You mean you'll hold the lines."

"No, sir. I can drive if I have a chance."

"That's what the American girl is saying these days. She wants to hold the lines."

"Well, I'm going to begin right now and drive all the way home."

As they drove off she flashed a roguish glance back at Arthur—a smile which shadowed swiftly into a look which had a certain appeal in it. He was very handsome in his working dress.

All the rest of the day that look was with him. He could not understand it, though her mood while seated upon the porch was perfectly comprehensible to him.

The following Sunday morning he saddled up one of the horses and went down to church. He reasoned Edith would attend the Episcopal service, and he had the pleasure of seeing her pass up the aisle most exquisitely dressed.

This feeling of pleasure was turned to sadness by sober second thought. Added to the prostration before his ideal was the feeling that she belonged to another world—a world of pleasure and wealth, a world without work or worry. This feeling was strengthened by the atmosphere of the beautiful little church, fragrant with flowers, delicately shadowed, tremulous with music.

He rode home in deep meditation. It was curious how subjective he was becoming. She had not seen him there, and his trip lacked so much of being a success. Life seemed hardly worth living as he took off his best suit and went out to feed the horses.

The men soon observed the regularity of these Sunday excursions, and the word was passed around that Arthur went down to see his girl, and they set themselves to find out who she was. They did not suspect that he sought the Major's niece.

It was a keen delight to see her, even at that distance. To get one look from her, or to see her eyelashes fall over her brown eyes, paid him for all his trouble, and yet it left him hungrier at heart than before.

Sometimes he got seated in such wise that he could see the fine line of her cheek and chin. He noticed also her growing color. The free life she lived in the face of the mountain winds was doing her good.

Sometimes he went at night to the song service, and his rides home alone on the plain, with the shadowy mountains over there massed in the starlit sky, were most wonderful experiences.

As he rose and fell on his broncho's steady gallop, he took off his hat to let the wind stir his hair. Riding thus, exalted thus, one night he shaped a desperate resolution. He determined to call on her just as he used to visit the girls at Viroqua with whom he was on the same intimacy of footing.

He was as good as any class. He was not as good as she was, for he lacked her sweetness and purity of heart, but merely the fact that she lived in a great house and wore beautiful garments, did not exclude him from calling upon her.

IV

But week after week went by without his daring to make his resolution good. He determined many times to ask permission to call, but somehow he never did.

He seemed to see her rather less than at first; and, on her part, there was a change. She seemed to have lost her first eager and frank curiosity about him, and did not always smile now when she met him.

Then, again, he could not in working dress ask to call; it would seem so incongruous to stand before her to make such a request covered with perspiration and dust. It was hard to be dignified under such circumstances; he must be washed and dressed properly.

In the meantime, the men had discovered how matters stood, and some of them made very free with the whole situation. Two of them especially hated him.

These two men had drifted to the farm from the mines somewhere, and were rough, hard characters. They would have come to blows with him, only they knew something of the power lying coiled in his long arms.

One day he overheard one of the men speaking of Edith, and his tone stopped the blood in Arthur's heart. When he walked among the group of men his face was white and set.

"You take that back!" he said in a low voice. "You take that back, or I'll kill you right where you stand!"

"Do him up, Tim!" shouted the other ruffian; but Tim hesitated. "I'll do him, then," said the other man. "I owe him one myself."

He caught up a strip of board which was lying on the ground near, but one of the Norwegian workmen put his foot on it, and before he could command his weapon, Arthur brought a pail which he held in his right hand down upon his opponent's head.

The man fell as if dead, and the pail shattered into its original staves. Arthur turned then to face Tim, his hands doubled into mauls; but the other men interfered, and the encounter was over.

Arthur waited to see if the fallen man could rise, and then turned away reeling and breathless. For an hour afterward his hands shook so badly that he could not go on with his work.

At first he determined to go to Richards, the foreman, and demand the discharge of the two tramps, but as he thought of the explanation necessary, he gave it up as impossible.

He almost wept with shame and despair at the thought of her name having been mixed in the tumult. He had meant to kill when he struck, and the nervous prostration which followed showed him how far he had gone. He had not had a fight since he was thirteen years of age, and now everything seemed lost in the light of his murderous rage. It would all come out sooner or later, and she would despise him.

He went to see the man just before going to supper, and found him in his barracks, sitting near a pail of cold water from which he was splashing his head at intervals.

He looked up as Arthur entered, but went on with his ministrations; after a pause he said:

Hamlin Garland

"That was a terrible lick you give me, young feller—brought the blood out of my ears."

"I meant to kill you," was Arthur's grim reply.

"I know you did. If that darned Norse hadn't put his foot on that board *you'd* be doing this." He lifted a handful of water to his swollen and aching head.

"What did you go to that board for? Why didn't you stand up like a man?"

"Because you were swinging that bucket."

"Oh, bosh! You were a coward as well as a blackguard."

The man looked up with a gleam in his eye.

"See here, young feller—if this head—"

Arthur's face darkened, and the man stopped short.

"Now listen, Dan Williams, I want to tell you something. I'm not going to report this. I'm going to let you stay here till you're well, and then I want this thing settled with Richards looking on; when I get through with you, then, you'll want a cot in some hospital."

The man's eyes sullenly fell, and Arthur turned toward the door. At the doorway he turned and a terrible look came into his face.

"And, more than that, if you say another word about—her, I'll brain you, sick or well!"

As he talked, the old, wild fury returned, and he came back

and faced the wounded man.

"Now, what do you propose to do?" he demanded, his hands clinching.

The other man looked at him, with a curious frown upon his face.

"Think I'm a damned fool!" he curtly answered, and sopped his handkerchief in the water again.

The rage went out of Arthur's eyes, and he almost smiled, so much did that familiar phrase convey, with its subtle inflections. It was cunning and candid and chivalrous all at once. It acknowledged defeat and guilt and embodied a certain pride in the victor.

"Well, that settles that," said Arthur. "One thing more—I don't want you to say what made the row between us."

"All right, pard; only, you'd better see Tim."

In spite of his care, the matter came to the ears of Richards, who laughed over it and told his wife, who stared blankly.

"Good land! When did it happen?"

"A couple of days ago."

"Wal, there! I thought there was a nigger in the fence. Dan had a head on him like a bushel basket. What was it about?"

"Something Tim said about Edith."

"I want to know! Wal, wal! An' here they've been going around as peaceful as two kittens ever since."

"Of course. They pitched in and settled it man fashion; they ain't a couple of women who go around sniffin' and spittin' at each other," said Richards, with brutal sarcasm. "As near as I can learn, Tim and Dan come at him to once."

"They're a nice pair of tramps!" said Mrs. Richards indignantly. "I told you when they come they'd make trouble."

"I told you the cow'd eat up the grindstone," Richards replied with a grin, walking away.

The more Mrs. Richards thought of it, the finer it all appeared to her. She was deeply engaged now on Arthur's side, and was very eager to do something to help on in his "sparking," as she called it. She seized the first opportunity to tell Edith.

"Don't s'pose you heard of the little fracas we had t'other day," she began, in phrase which she intended to be delicately indirect.

Edith was sitting in the cart, and Mrs. Richards stood at the wheel, with her apron shading her head.

"Why, no. What was it?"

"Mr. Ramsey come mighty near gettin' killed." The old woman enjoyed deeply the dramatic pallor and distortion of the girl's face.

"Why—why—what do you mean?"

"Wal, if he hadn't a lammed one feller with a bucket he'd a been laid out sure. So Richards says; as it is, it's the other feller that has the head." She laughed to see the girl's face grow rosy again.

"Then—Mr. Ramsey isn't hurt?"

"Not a scratch! The funny part of it is, they've been going around here for a week, quiet as you please. I wouldn't have known anything about it only for Richards."

"Oh, isn't it dreadful?" said the girl.

"Yes, 'tis!" the elder woman readily agreed; "but why don't you ask what it was all about?"

"Oh, I don't want to know anything more about it; it's too terrible."

Mrs. Richards was approaching the climax.

"It was all about you."

The girl could not realize what part she should have with a disgraceful row in the barnyard of her uncle's farm.

"Yes, these men—they're regular tramps; I told Richards so the first time I set eyes on 'em—they made a little free with your name, and Art he overheard them and he went for 'em, and they both come at him, two to one, and he lammed both out in a minute—so Richards says. Now I call that splendid; don't you? A young feller that'll stand up for his girl ag'in two big tramps—"

The Major had been motioning for Edith to drive on down toward the gate, and she seized the chance for escape. Her lips quivered with shame and anger. It seemed already as if she had been splashed with mire.

"Oh, the vulgar creatures!" she said, in her throat, her teeth shut tight.

"There, isn't that a fine field?" asked the Major, as he pointed to the cabbages. "There is a chance for an American imitator of Monet—those purple-brown deeps and those gray-blue-pink pearl tints—What's the matter, my dear?" he broke off to ask. "Are you ill?"

"No, no, only let's go home," she said, the tears coming into her eyes.

He got in hastily.

"My dear, you are really ill. What's the matter? Has your old enemy the headache—" He put his arm about her tenderly.

"No, no! I'm sick of this place—I wish I'd never seen it! How could those dreadful men fight about me? It's horrible!"

The Major whistled.

"Oh, ho! that's got around to you, has it? I didn't know it myself until yesterday; I was hoping it wouldn't reach you at all. I wouldn't mind it, my dear. It's the shadow every lovely woman throws, no matter where she walks; it's only your shadow that has passed over the cesspool."

"But I can't even bear that; it seems like a part of me. What do you suppose they said of me?" she asked, in morbid curiosity.

"Now, now, dearest, to know that would be stepping into the muck after your shadow; the talk of such men is unimaginable to you."

"You don't mean Mr. Ramsey?"

"No; Mr. Ramsey is a different sort of man, and I don't

suppose anything else would have brought him to blows with those rough men."

They sat looking straight forward.

"Oh, it's horrible, horrible!"

Her uncle tightened his arm about her.

"I suppose the knowledge of such lower deeps must come to you some day, but don't seek it now; I've told you all you ought to know. Ramsey meant well," he went on, after a silence, "but such things do little good, not enough to pay for the outlay of self-respect. He can't control their talk when he's out of hearing."

"But I supposed that if a woman was—good—I mean—I didn't know that men talked in that way about girls—like me. How could they?"

The abyss still fascinated her.

"My dear, such men are only half civilized. They have all the passions of animals, and all the vices of men. Ramsey was too hot-headed; their words do not count; they weren't worth whipping."

There was a little silence. They were nearing the mountains again, and both raised their eyes to the peaks deeply shadowed in Tyrian purple.

"I know how you feel, I think," the Major went on, "but the best thing to do is to forget it. I'm sorry Ramsey fought. To walk into a gang of rough men like that is foolish and dangerous too, for the ruffian is generally the best man physically, I'm sorry to say."

Hamlin Garland

"It was brave, though, don't you think so?" she asked.

He looked at her quickly.

"Oh, yes; it was brave and very youthful."

She smiled a little for the first time.

"I guess I like youth."

"In that case I'll have to promote him for it," he said with a smile that made her look away toward the mountains again.

V

Saulisbury took a sudden turn to friendliness, and defended the action when the Major related the story that night at the dinner table, as they were seated over their coffee and cigars. He was dining with the Saulisburys.

"It's uncommon plucky, that's what I think, d'ye kneow. By Jeove, I didn't think the young dog had it in him, really. He did one fellow up with a bucket, they say, and met the other fellow with his left. Where did the young beggah get his science?"

"At college, I suppose."

"But I suppeosed these little Western colleges were a milk-and-wahta sawt of thing, ye kneow—Baptist and Christian Endeavor, and all that, ye kneow."

"Oh, no," laughed the Major. "They are not so benighted as that. They give a little attention to the elementary studies, though I believe athletics do come second on the curriculum."

"Well, the young dog seems to have made some use of his chawnce," said Saulisbury, who had dramatized the matter in his own way, and saw Ramsey doing the two men up in accordance with Queensberry rules. "I wouldn't hawf liked the jobe meself, do ye kneow. They're forty years apiece, and as hard as nails."

Mrs. Saulisbury looked up from her walnuts.

"Sam is ready to carry the olive club to Mr. Ramsey. 'The poor beggar,' as he has called him all along, will be a gentleman from this time forward."

After the Major had gone, Saulisbury said:

"There's one thing the Majah was careful note to mention, my deah. Why should this young fellow be going abeout defending the good name of his niece? Do ye kneow, my deah, I fancy the young idiot is in love with her."

"Well, suppose he is?"

"But, my deah! In England, you kneow, it wouldn't mattah; it would be a case of hopeless devotion. But as I understand things heah, it may become awkward. Don't ye think so, love?"

"It depends upon the young man. Edith could do worse than marry a good, clean, wholesome fellow like that."

"Good gracious! You deon't allow your mind to go that fah?"

"Why, certainly! I'd much rather she'd marry a strong young workingman than some burnt-out third-generation wreck of her own set in the city."

"But the fellow has no means."

"He has muscle and brains, and besides, she has something of her own."

Saulisbury filled his pipe slowly.

"Luckily, it's all theory on our part; the contingency isn't heah—isn't likely to arrive, in fact."

"Don't be too sure. If I can read a girl's heart in the lines of her face, she's got where principalities and powers are of small account."

"Really?"

"Sure as shooting," she smilingly said.

Saulisbury mused and puffed.

"In that case, we will have to turn in and give the fellow what you Americans call a boost."

"That's *right*," his wife replied slangily.

Edith went to her room that night with a mind whirling in dizzying circles, whose motion she could not check. It was terrible to have it all come in this way.

She knew Arthur cared for her—she had known it from the first—but with the happy indifference of youth, she had not looked forward to the end of the summer. The sure outcome of passion had kept itself somewhere in a golden glimmer on the lower sweep of the river.

She wished for some one to go to for advice. Mrs. Thayer, she knew, would exclaim in horror over the matter. The Major had hinted the course she would have to take, which was to show Arthur he had no connection with her life—if she could. But deep in her heart she knew she could not do that.

Suddenly a thought came to her which made her flush till the dew of shame stood upon her forehead. He had never been to see her; she had always been to see him!

She knew that this was true. She did not attempt to conceal it from herself now. The charm of those rides with her uncle was the chance of seeing Arthur. The sweet, never-wearying charm that made this summer one of perfect happiness, that had made her almost forget her city ways and friends, that had made her brown and strong with the soil and wind, was daily contact with a robust and wholesome young man, a sturdy figure with brown throat and bare, strong arms.

She went off at this point into a retrospective journey along the pathways of her summer outing. At this place he stood at the watering trough, leaning upon his great gray horse. Here he was walking behind his plow; he was lifting his hat—the clear sunshine fell over his face. She saw again the splendid flex of his side and powerful thigh. Here he was in the hayfield, and she saw the fork-handle bend like a willow twig under his smiling effort, the muscles on his brown arms rolling like some perfect machinery. She idealized all he did, and the entire summer and the wide landscape seemed filled with prismatic colors.

Then her self-accusations came back. She had gone down into the field to see him; perhaps the very man who was with him then was one of those who had jested of her and whom he had punished. Her little hands clutched.

"I'll never go out there again! I'll never see him again—never!" she said, with her teeth shut tight.

Mrs. Thayer did not take any very great interest in the matter until Mrs. Saulisbury held a session with her. Then she sputtered in deep indignation.

"Why, how dare he make love to my niece? Why, the presumptuous thing! Why, the idea! He's a workingman!"

Mrs. Saulisbury remained calm and smiling. She was the only person who could manage Mrs. Thayer.

"Yes, that's true. But he's a college-bred man, and—"

"College-bred! These nasty little Western colleges—what do they amount to? Why, he curries our horses."

Mrs. Saulisbury was amused.

"I know that is an enormity, but I heard the Major tell of currying horses once."

"That was in the army—anyhow, it doesn't matter. Edith can simply ignore the whole thing."

"I hope she can, but I doubt it very much."

"What do you mean?"

"I mean that Edith is interested in him."

"I don't believe it! Why, it is impossible! You're crazy, Jeannette!"

"He's very handsome in a way."

"He's red and big-jointed, and he's a common plowboy." Mrs. Thayer gasped, returning to her original charge.

Mrs. Saulisbury laughed, being malevolent enough to enjoy the whole situation.

"He appears to me to be a very uncommon plowboy. Well, I wouldn't try to do anything about it, Charlotte," she added. "You remember the fate of the Brookses, who tried to force Maud to give up her clerk. If this is a case of true love, you might as well surrender gracefully."

"But I can't do that. I'm responsible for her to her father. I'll go right straight and ask her."

"Charlotte," Mrs. Saulisbury's voice rang with a stern note, "don't you *presume* to do such a thing! You will precipitate everything. The girl don't know her own mind, and if you go up there and attack this young man, you'll tip the whole dish over. Don't you know you can't safely abuse that young fellow in her hearing? Sit down now and be reasonable. Leave her alone for a while. Let her think it over alone."

This good counsel prevailed, and the other woman settled into a calmer state.

"Well, it's a dreadful thing, anyhow."

"Perfectly dreadful! But you mustn't take a conventional view of it. You must remember, a good, handsome, healthy man should come first as a husband, and this young man is very attractive, and I must admit he seems a gentleman, so far as I can see. Besides, you can't do anything by storming up to that poor girl. Let her alone for a few days."

Following this suggestion, no one alluded to the fight, or appeared to notice Edith's changed moods, but Mrs. Saulisbury could not forbear giving her an occasional squeeze of wordless sympathy, as she passed her.

It was pitiful to see the tumult and fear and responsibility of the world coming upon this dainty, simple-hearted girl. Life had been so straightforward before. No toil, no problems, no choosing of things for one's self. Now suddenly here was the greatest problem of all coming at the end of a summer-time outing.

Meanwhile Arthur was longing to see Edith once more, and wondering why she had stopped coming.

The Major came up on Friday and Saturday, but came alone,

and that left only the hope of seeing Edith at church, and the young fellow worked on with that to nerve his arm.

The family respected his departure on Sunday. They plainly felt his depression, and sympathized with it.

"Walk home with her. I would," said Mrs. Richards, as he went through the kitchen.

"So would I. Dang me if I'd stand off," Richards started to say, but Arthur did not stop to listen.

As he rode down to the city, he recovered, naturally, a little of his buoyancy. Sleep had rested his body and cleared his mind for action.

He sat in his usual place at the back of the church, and his heart throbbed painfully as he saw her moving up the aisle, a miracle of lace and coolness, with fragrant linen enveloping her lovely young form, so erect and graceful and slender.

Then his heart bowed down before her, not because she was above him in a social class—he did not admit that—but because he was a lover, and she was his ideal. He was cast down as suddenly as he had been exalted by her timid look around, as was her custom, in order to bow to him.

He stood at the door as they came out, though he felt foolish and boyish in doing so. She approached him with eyes turned away; but as she passed him she flashed an appealing, mystical look at him, and, flushing a radiant pink, slipped out of the side door, leaving him stunned and smarting for a moment.

As he mounted his horse and rode away toward the ranch, his thoughts were busy with that strange look of hers. He came to understand and to believe at last that she appealed to him and trusted in him and waited for him.

Then something strong and masterful rose in him. He lifted his big brown fist in the air in a resolution which was like that of Napoleon when he entered Russia. He turned and rode furiously back toward the town.

As he walked up the gravel path to the Thayer house it seemed like a castle to him. The great granite portico, the curving flight of steps, the splendor of the glass above the door, all impressed him with the terrible gulf between his fortune and hers.

He was met at the door by the girl from the table. He greeted her as his equal, and said:

"Is Miss Newell at home?"

The girl smiled with perfect knowledge and sympathy. She was on his side; and she knew, besides, how much it meant to have the hired man come in at the front door.

"Yes, she's at dinner. Won't you come in, Mr. Ramsey?"

He entered without further words, and followed her into the reception room, which was the most splendid room he had ever seen. He stood with his feet upon a rug which was worth more than his year's pay, and he knew it.

"Just take a seat here, and I'll announce you," said the girl, who was almost trembling with eagerness to explode her torpedo of news.

"Don't disturb them. I'll wait."

But she had whisked out of the room, having plans of her own; perhaps revenges of her own.

Arthur listened. He could not help it. He heard the girl's clear, distinct voice; the open doorways conveyed every word to him.

"It's Mr. Ramsey, ma'am, to see Miss Newell."

The young man's strained ears heard the sudden pause in the click of knives and plates. He divined the gasps of astonishment with which Mrs. Thayer's utterance began.

"Well, I declare! Now, Major, you see what I told you?"

"The plucky young dog!" said Saulisbury, in sincere admiration.

Mrs. Thayer went on:

"Now, Mr. Thayer, this is the result of treating your servants as equals."

The Major laughed.

"My dear, you're a little precipitate. It may be a mistake. The young man may be here to tell me one of the colts is sick."

"You don't believe any such thing! You heard what the girl said—Oh, look at Edith!"

There was a sudden pushing and scraping of chairs. Arthur rose, tense, terrified. A little flurry of voices followed.

"Here, give her some wine! The poor thing! No wonder—"

Then a slight pause.

"She's all right," said the Major in a relieved tone. "Just a little surprised, that's all."

There came a little inarticulate murmur from the girl, and then another pause.

"By Jove! this is getting dramatic!" said Saulisbury.

"Be quiet, Sam," said his wife. "I won't have any of your scoffing. I'm glad there is some sincerity of emotion left in our city girls."

Mrs. Thayer broke in:

"Major, you go right out there and send that impudent creature away. It's disgraceful!"

Arthur turned cold and hard as granite. His heart rose with a murderous, slow swell. He held his breath, while the calm, amused voice of the Major replied:

"But, see here, my dear, it's none of my business. Mr. Ramsey is an American citizen—I like him—he has a perfect right to call—"

"H'yah, h'yah!" called Saulisbury in a chuckle.

"He's a man of parts, and besides, I rather imagine Edith has given him the right to call."

The anger died out of Arthur's heart, and the warm blood rushed once more through his tingling body. Tears came to his eyes, and he could have embraced his defender.

"Nothing like consistency, Majah," said Saulisbury.

"Sam, will you be quiet?"

The Major went on:

"I imagine the whole matter is for Edith to decide. It's really very simple. Let her send word to him that she does not care to see him, and he'll go away—no doubt of it."

"Why, of course," said Mrs. Thayer. "Edith, just tell Mary to say to Mr. What's-his-name—"

Again that creeping thrill came into the young man's hair. His world seemed balanced on a needle's point.

Then a chair was pushed back slowly. There was another little flurry. Again the blood poured over him like a splash of warm water, leaving him cold and wet.

"Edith!" called the astonished, startled voice of Mrs. Thayer. "What are you going to do?"

"I'm going to see him," said the girl's firm voice.

There was a soft clapping of two pairs of hands.

As she came through the portiere, Edith walked like a princess. There was amazing resolution in her back-flung head, and on her face was the look of one who sets sail into unknown seas.

Someway—somehow, through a mist of light and a blur of sound, he met her—and the cling of her arms about his neck moved him to tears.

No word was uttered till the Major called from the doorway:

"Mr. Ramsey, Mrs. Thayer wants to know if you won't come and have some dinner."

A STOP-OVER AT TYRE

I

Albert Lohr was studying the motion of the ropes and lamps, and listening to the rumble of the wheels and the roar of the ferocious wind against the pane of glass that his head touched. It was the midnight train from Marion rushing toward Warsaw like some savage thing unchained, creaking, shrieking, and clattering through the wild storm which possessed the whole Mississippi Valley.

Albert lost sight of the lamps at last, and began to wonder what his future would be. "First I must go through the university at Madison; then I'll study law, go into politics, and perhaps some time I may go to Washington."

In imagination he saw that wonderful city. As a Western boy, Boston to him was historic, New York was the great metropolis, but Washington was the great American city, and political greatness the only fame.

The car was nearly empty: save here and there the wide-awake Western drummer, and a woman with four fretful children, the train was as deserted as it was frightfully cold. The engine shrieked warningly at intervals, the train rumbled

Hamlin Garland

hollowly over short bridges and across pikes, swung round the hills, and plunged with wild warnings past little towns hid in the snow, with only here and there a light shining dimly.

One of the drummers now and then rose up from his cramped bed on the seats, and swore dreadfully at the railway company for not heating the cars. The woman with the children inquired for the tenth time, "Is the next station Lodi?"

"Yes, ma'am, it is," snarled the drummer, as he jerked viciously at the strap on his valise; "and darned glad I am, too, I can tell yeh! I'll be stiff as a car-pin if I stay in this infernal ice chest another hour. I wonder what the company think—"

At Lodi several people got on, among them a fat man and his pretty daughter abnormally wide awake considering the time of night. She saw Albert for the same reason that he saw her—they were both young and good-looking.

He began his musings again, modified by this girl's face. He had left out the feminine element; obviously he must recapitulate. He'd study law, yes; but that would not prevent going to sociables and church fairs. And at these fairs the chances were good for a meeting with a girl. Her father must be influential—country judge or district attorney; this would open new avenues.

He was roused by the sound of his own name.

"Is Albert Lohr in this car?" shouted the brakeman, coming in, enveloped in a cloud of fine snow.

"Yes, here!" shouted Albert.

"Here's a telegram for you."

Albert snatched the envelope with a sudden fear of disaster at home; but it was dated "Tyre":

> "Get off at Tyre. I'll be there.
> "Hartley."

"Well, now, that's fun!" said Albert, looking at the brakeman. "When do we reach there?"

"About 2.20."

"Well, by thunder! A pretty time o' night!"

The brakeman grinned sympathetically. "Any answer?" he asked at length.

"No; that is, none that 'u'd do the matter justice," Albert said, studying the telegram.

"Hartley friend o' yours?"

"Yes; know him?"

"Yes; he boarded where I did in Warsaw."

When he came back again, the brakeman said to Albert, in a hesitating way:

"Ain't going t' stop off long, I s'pose?"

"May an' may not; depends on Hartley. Why?"

"Well, I've got an aunt there that keeps boarders, and I kind o' like t' send her one when I can. If you should happen to stay a few days, go an' see her. She sets up first-class grub, an' it wouldn't kill anybody, anyhow, if you went up an' called."

"Course not. If I stay long enough to make it pay I'll look her up sure. I ain't no Vanderbilt to stop at two-dollar-a-day hotels."

The brakeman sat down opposite Albert, encouraged by his smile.

"Y' see, my division ends at Warsaw, and I run back and forth here every other day, but I don't get much chance to see them, and I ain't worth a cuss f'r letter-writin'. Y'see, she's only aunt by marriage, but I like her; an' I guess she's got about all she can stand up under, an' so I like t' help her a little when I can. The old man died owning nothing but the house, an' that left the old lady t' rustle f'r her livin'. Dummed if she ain't sandy as old Sand. They're gitt'n' along purty—"

The whistle blew for brakes, and, seizing his lantern, the brakeman slammed out on the platform.

"Tough night for twisting brakes," suggested Albert, when he came in again.

"Yes—on the freight."

"Good heavens! I should say so. They don't run freight such nights as this?"

"Don't they? Well, I guess they don't stop for a storm like this if they's any money to be made by sending her through. Many's the night I've broke all night on top of the old wooden cars, when the wind cut like a razor. Shear the hair off a cast-iron mule—*woo-o-o*! There's where you need grit, old man," he ended, dropping into familiar speech.

"Yes; or need a job awful bad."

The brakeman was struck with this idea. "There's where you're right. A fellow don't take that kind of a job for the fun of it. Not much! He takes it because he's got to. That's as sure's you're a foot high. I tell you, a feller's got t' rustle these days if he gits any kind of a job—"

"*Toot, too-o-o-o-t, toot!*"

The station passed, the brakeman did not return, perhaps because he found some other listener, perhaps because he was afraid of boring this pleasant young fellow. Albert shuddered with a sympathetic pain as he thought of the men on the tops of the icy cars, with hands straining at the brake, and the wind cutting their faces like a sand-blast. His mind went out to the thousands of freight trains shuttling to and fro across the vast web of gleaming iron spread out on the mighty breast of the Western plains. Oh, those tireless hands at the wheel and throttle!

He looked at his watch; it was two o'clock; the next station was Tyre. As he began to get his things together, the brakeman came in.

"Oh, I forgot to say that the old lady's name is Welsh—Mrs. Robert Welsh. Say I sent yeh, and it'll be all right."

"Sure! I'll try her in the morning—that is, if I find out I'm going to stay."

"Tyre! *Tyre!*" yelled the brakeman, as with clanging bell and whizz of steam the train slowed down and the wheels began to cry out in the snow.

Albert got his things together, and pulled his cap firmly down on his head.

"Here goes!" he muttered.

"Hold y'r breath!" shouted the brakeman. Albert swung himself to the platform before the station—a platform of planks along which the snow was streaming like water.

"Good night!" called the brakeman.

"*Good* night!"

"All-l abo-o-o-ard!" called the conductor somewhere in the storm; the brakeman swung his lantern, and the train drew off into the blinding whirl, and the lights were soon lost in the clouds of snow.

No more desolate place could well be imagined. A level plain, apparently bare of houses, swept by a ferocious wind; a dingy little den called a station—no other shelter in sight; no sign of life save the dull glare of two windows to the left, alternately lost and found in the storm.

Albert's heart contracted with a sudden fear; the outlook was appalling.

"Where's the town?" he yelled savagely at a dimly seen figure with a lantern—a man evidently locking the station door, his only refuge.

"Over there," was the surly reply.

"How far?"

"'Bout a mile."

"A mile!"

"That's what I said—a mile."

"Well, I'll be blanked!"

"Well, y'better be doing something besides standing here, 'r y' 'll freeze t' death. I'd go over to the Arteeshun House an' go t' bed if I was in your fix."

"Oh, y' would!"

"I would."

"Well, where *is* the Artesian House?"

"See them lights?"

"I see them lights."

"Well, they're it."

"Oh, wouldn't your grammar make Old Grammati-cuss curl up, though!"

"What say?" queried the man, bending his head toward Albert, his form being almost lost in the snow that streamed against them both.

"I said I guessed I'd try it," grinned the youth invisibly.

"Well, I would if I was in your fix. Keep right close after me; they's some ditches here, and the foot-bridges are none too wide."

"The Artesian is owned by the railway, eh?"

"Yup."

"And you're the clerk?"

"Yup; nice little scheme, ain't it?"

"Well, it'll do," replied Albert.

The man laughed without looking around.

"Keep your longest cuss words till morning; you'll need 'em, take my word for it."

In the little barroom, lighted by a vilely smelling kerosene lamp, the clerk, hitherto a shadow and a voice, came to light as a middle-aged man with a sullen face slightly belied by a sly twinkle in his eyes.

"This beats all the winters I ever *did* see. It don't do nawthin' but blow, *blow*. Want to go to bed, I s'pose. Well, come along."

He took up one of the absurd little lamps and tried to get more light out of it.

"Dummed if a white bean wouldn't be better."

"Spit on it!" suggested Albert.

"I'd throw the whole business out o' the window for a cent," growled the man.

"Here's y'r cent," said the boy.

"You're mighty frisky f'r a feller gitt'n' off'n a midnight train," replied the man, tramping along a narrow hallway, and talking in a voice loud enough to awaken every sleeper in the house.

"Have t' be, or there'd be a pair of us."

"You'll laugh out o' the other side o' y'r mouth when you saw away on one o' the bell-collar steaks this house puts up," ended the clerk as he put the lamp down.

"'Sufficient unto the day is the evil thereof,'" called Albert after him, and then plunged into the icy bed.

He was awakened the next morning by the cooks pounding steak down in the kitchen and wrangling over some division of duty. It was a vile place at any time, but on a morning like this it was appalling. The water was frozen, the floor like ice, the seven-by-nine glass frosted so that he couldn't see to comb his hair.

"All that got me out of bed," said Albert to the clerk, "was the thought of leaving."

"Got y'r teeth filed?" said the day clerk, with a wink. "Old Collins's beef will try 'em."

The breakfast was incredibly bad—so much worse than he expected that Albert was forced to admit he had never seen its like. He fled from the place without a glance behind, and took passage in an omnibus for the town, a mile away. It was terribly cold, the thermometer twenty below zero; but the sun was very brilliant, and the air still.

The driver pulled up before a very ambitious wooden hotel entitled "The Eldorado," and Albert dashed in at the door and up to the stove, with both hands covering his ears.

As he stood there, frantic with pain, kicking his toes and rubbing his ears, he heard a chuckle—a slow, sly, insulting chuckle—turned, and saw Hartley standing in the doorway, visibly exulting over his misery.

"Hello, Bert! that you?"

"What's left of me. Say, you're a good one, you are? Why didn't you telegraph me at Marion? A deuce of a night I've had of it!"

"Do ye good," laughed Hartley, a tall, alert, handsome fellow nearly thirty years of age.

After a short and vigorous "blowing up," Albert said: "Well, now, what's the meaning of all this, anyhow? Why this change from Racine?"

"Well, you see, I got wind of another fellow going to work this county for a 'Life of Logan,' and thinks I, 'By jinks! I'd better drop in ahead of him with Blaine's "Twenty Years."' I telegraphed f'r territory, got it, and telegraphed to stop you."

"You did it. When did you come down?"

"Last night, six o'clock."

Albert was getting warmer and better-natured.

"Well, I'm here; what ye going t'do with me?"

"I'll use you some way; can't tell. First thing is to find a boarding place where we can work in a couple o' books on the bill."

"Well, I don't know about that, but I'm going to look up a

place a brakeman gave me a pointer on."

"All right; here goes!"

Scarcely any one was stirring on the streets. The wind was pitilessly cold, though not strong. The snow under the feet cried out with a note like glass and steel. The windows of the stores were thick with frost, and Albert gave a shudder of fear, almost as if he were homeless. He had never experienced anything like it before.

Entering one of the stores, they found a group of men sitting about the stove, smoking, chatting, and spitting aimlessly into a huge spittoon made of boards and filled with sawdust. Each man suspended smoking and talking as the strangers entered.

"Can any of you gentlemen tell us where Mrs. Welsh lives?"

There was a silence; then the clerk behind the counter said:

"I guess so. Two blocks north and three west, next to last house on left-hand side."

"Clear as a bell!" laughed Hartley, and they pushed out into the cold again, drawing their mufflers up to their eyes.

"I don't want much of this," muttered Bert through his scarf.

The house was a large frame house standing on the edge of a bank, and as the young men waited they could look down on the meadow land, where the river lay blue and still and as hard as iron.

A pale little girl ten, or twelve years of age, let them in.

"Is this where Mrs. Welsh lives?"

"Yes, sir."

"Will you ask her to come here a moment?"

"Yes, sir," piped the little one. "Won't you sit down by the fire?" she added, with a quaint air of hospitality.

The room was the usual village sitting room: a cylinder heater full of wood at one side of it; a rag carpet, much faded, on the floor; a cabinet organ; a doleful pair of crayon portraits on the wall, one supposedly a baby—a figure dressed like a child of six months, but with a face old and cynical enough to be forty-five. The paper on the wall was of the hideous striped sort, and the chairs were nondescript; but everything was clean—so clean it looked worn more with brushing than with use.

A slim woman of fifty, with hollow eyes and a patient smile, came in, wiping her hands on her apron.

"How d'ye do? Did you want to see me?"

"Yes," said Hartley, smiling. "The fact is, we're book agents, and looking for a place to board."

"Well—a—I—yes, I keep boarders."

"I was sent here by a brakeman on the midnight express," put in Bert.

"Oh, Tom," said the woman, her face clearing. "Tom's always sending us people. Why, yes; I've got room for you, I guess—this room here." She pushed open a folding door leading into what had been her parlor.

"You can have this."

"And the price?"

"Four dollars."

"Eight dollars f'r the two of us. All right; we'll be with you a week or two if we have luck."

The woman smiled and shut the door. Bert thought how much she looked like his mother in the back—the same tired droop in the shoulders, the same colorless dress, once blue or brown, now a peculiar drab, characterless with much washing.

"Excuse me, won't you? I've got to be at my baking; make y'rselves at home."

"Now, Jim," said Bert, "I'm going t' stay right here while you go and order our trunks around—just t' pay you off f'r last night."

"All right," said Hartley, cheerily going out. After getting warm, Bert sat down at the organ and played a gospel hymn or two from the Moody and Sankey hymnal. He was in the midst of the chorus of "Let your lower lights," etc., when a young woman entered the room. She had a whisk-broom in her hand, and stood a picture of gentle surprise. Bert wheeled about on his stool.

"I thought it was Stella," she began.

"I'm a book agent," said Bert, rising with his best grace; "I might as well out with it. I'm here to board."

"Oh!" said the girl, with some relief. She was very fair and very slight, almost frail. Her eyes were of the sunniest blue, her face pale and somewhat thin, but her lips showed scarlet, and her teeth were fine. Bert liked her and smiled.

"A book agent is the next thing to a burglar, I know; but still—"

"Oh, I didn't mean that, but I *was* surprised. When did you come?"

"Just a few moments ago. Am I in your way?" he inquired, with elaborate solicitude.

"Oh, no! Please go on; you play very well, I think. It is so seldom young men play."

"I had to at college; the other fellows all wanted to sing. You play, of course."

"When I have time." She sighed. There was a weary droop in her voice; she seemed aware of it, and said more brightly:

"You mean Marion, I suppose?"

"Yes; I'm in my second year."

"I went there two years. Then I had to quit and come home to help mother."

"Did you? That's why I'm out here on this infernal book business—to get money."

She looked at him with interest now, noticing his fine eyes and waving brown hair.

"It's dreadful, isn't it? But you've got a hope to go back. I haven't. At first I didn't think I could live; but I did." She ended with a sigh, a far-off expression in her eyes.

There was a pause again. Bert felt that she was no ordinary girl, and she was quite as strongly drawn to him.

"It almost killed me to give it up. I don't s'pose I'd know any of the scholars you know. Even the teachers are not the same. Oh, yes—Sarah Shaw; I think she's back for the normal course."

"Oh, yes!" exclaimed Bert, "I know Sarah. We boarded on the same street; used t' go home together after class. An awful nice girl, too."

"She's a worker. She teaches school. I can't do that, for mother needs me at home." There was another pause, broken by the little girl, who called:

"Maud, mamma wants you."

Maud rose and went out, with a tired smile on her face that emphasized her resemblance to her mother. Bert couldn't forget that smile, and he was still thinking about the girl, and what her life must be, when Hartley came in.

"By jinks! It's *snifty*, as dad used to say. You can't draw a long breath through your nostrils; freeze y'r nose solid as a bottle," he announced, throwing off his coat with an air which seemed to make him an old resident of the room.

"By the way, I've just found out why you was so anxious to get into this house, hey?" he said, slapping Bert's knee. "Another case o' girl."

Bert blushed; he couldn't help it, notwithstanding his

innocence in this case. Hartley went on.

"Oh, I know you! A girl in the house; might 'a' known it," Hartley continued, in a hoarse whisper.

"I didn't know it myself till about ten minutes ago," protested Bert.

Hartley winked prodigiously.

"Don't tell me! Is she pretty?"

"No—that is, *you* wouldn't call her so."

"Oh, the deuce I wouldn't! Don't you *wish* I wouldn't? I'd like to see the girl I wouldn't call pretty, right to her face, too."

The girl returned at this moment with an armful of wood.

"Let *me* put it in," cried Hartley, springing up. "Excuse me. My name is Hartley, book agent: Blaine's 'Twenty Years,' plain cloth, sprinkled edges, three dollars; half calf, three fifty. This is my friend Mr. Lohr, of Marion; German extraction, soph at the university."

The girl bowed and smiled, and pushed by him toward the door of the parlor. Hartley followed her in, and Bert could hear them rattling away at the stove.

"Won't you sit down and play for us?" asked Hartley, after they returned to the sitting room, with the persuasive music of the book agent in his fine voice.

"Oh, no! It's nearly dinner time, and I must help about the table."

"Now make yourselves at home," said Mrs. Welsh, appearing at the door leading to the kitchen; "if you want anything, just let me know."

"All right. We will; don't worry. We'll be trouble enough.— Nice people," said Hartley, as he shut the door of their room and sat down. "But the girl *ain't* what I call pretty."

By the time the dinner bell rang they were feeling at home in their new quarters. At the table they met the other boarders: the Brann brothers, newsdealers; old man Troutt, who kept the livery stable (and smelled of it); and a small, dark, and wizened woman who kept the millinery store. The others, who came in late, were clerks.

Maud served the dinner, while Stella and her mother waited upon the table. Albert was accustomed to this, and made little account of the service. He did notice the hands of the girl, however, so white and graceful; no amount of work could quite remove their essential shapeliness.

Hartley struck up a conversation with the newsdealers and left Bert free to observe Maud. She was not more than twenty, he decided, but she looked older, so careworn and sad was her face.

"They's one thing ag'in' yeh," Troutt, the liveryman, was bawling to Hartley: "they's jest been worked one o' the goldingedest schemes you *ever* see! 'Bout six munce ago s'm' fellers come all through here claimin' t' be after information about the county and the leadin' citizens; wanted t' write a history, an' wanted all the pitchers of the leading men, old settlers, an' so on. You paid ten dollars, an' you had a book an' your pitcher in it."

"I know the scheme," grinned Hartley.

"Wal, sir, I s'pose them fellers roped in every man in this town. I don't s'pose they got out with a cent less'n one thousand dollars. An' when the book come—wal!" Here he stopped to roar. "I don't s'pose you ever see a madder lot o' men in your life. In the first place, they got the names and the pitchers mixed so that I was Judge Ricker, an' Judge Ricker was ol' man Daggett. Didn't the judge swear—oh, it was awful!"

"I should say so."

"An' the pitchers that wa'n't mixed was so goldinged *black* you couldn't tell 'em from niggers. You know how kind o' lily-livered Lawyer Ransom is? Wal, he looked like ol' black Joe; he was the maddest man of the hull b'ilin'. He throwed the book in the fire, and tromped around like a blind bull."

"It wasn't a success, I take it, then. Why, I should 'a' thought they'd 'a' nabbed the fellows."

"Not much! They was too keen for that. They didn't deliver the books theirselves; they hired Dick Bascom to do it f'r them. Course Dick wa'n't t' blame."

"No; I never tried it before," Albert was saying to Maud, at their end of the table. "Hartley offered me a good thing to come, and as I needed money, I came. I don't know what he's going to do with me, now I'm here."

Albert did not go out after dinner with Hartley; it was too cold. Hartley let nothing stand in the way of business, however. He had been at school with Albert during his first year, but had gone back to work in preference to study.

Albert had brought his books with him, planning to keep up with his class, if possible, and was deep in a study of Caesar when he heard a timid knock on the door.

"Come!" he called, student fashion.

Maud entered, her face aglow.

"How natural that sounds!" she said.

Albert sprang up to help her put down the wood in her arms. "I wish you'd let me bring the wood," he said pleadingly, as she refused his aid.

"I wasn't sure you were in. Were you reading?"

"Caesar," he replied, holding up the book. "I am conditioned on Latin. I'm going over the 'Commentaries' again."

"I thought I knew the book," she laughed.

"You read Latin?"

"Yes, a little—Vergil."

"Maybe you can help me out on these *oratia obliqua*. They bother me yet. I hate these 'Caesar saids.' I like Vergil better."

She stood at his shoulder while he pointed out the knotty passage. She read it easily, and he thanked her. It was amazing how well acquainted they felt after this; they were as fellow-students.

The wind roared outside in the bare maples, and the fire boomed in its pent place within. The young people forgot the time and place. The girl sank into a chair almost unconsciously as they talked of Madison—a great city to them—of the Capitol building, of the splendid campus, of the lakes and the gay sailing there in summer and ice-boating in winter, of the struggles of "rooming."

"Oh, it makes me homesick!" cried the girl, with a deep sigh. "It was the happiest, sunniest time of all my life. Oh, those walks and talks! Those recitations in the dear, chalky old rooms! Oh, *how* I would like to go back over that hollow doorstone again!"

She broke off, with tears in her eyes. He was obliged to cough two or three times before he could break the silence.

"I know just how you feel. I know, the first spring when I went back on the farm, it seemed as if I couldn't stand it. I thought I'd go crazy. The days seemed forty-eight hours long. It was so lonesome, and so dreary on rainy days! But of course I expected to go back; that's what kept me up. I don't think I could have stood it if I hadn't had hope."

"I've given it up now," she said plaintively; "it's no use hoping."

"Why don't you teach?" asked Albert, deeply affected by her voice and manner.

"I did teach here for a year, but I couldn't endure the noise; I'm not very strong, and the boys were so rude. If I could teach in a seminary—teach Latin and English—I should be happy, I think. But I can't leave mother now."

She began to appear a different girl in the boy's eyes; the cheap dress, the check apron, could not hide her pure intellectual spirit. Her large blue eyes were deep with thought, and the pale face, lighted by the glow of the fire, was as lovely as a rose. Almost before he knew it, he was telling her of his life.

"I don't see how I endured it as long as I did," he went on. "It was nothing but work, work, and mud the whole year round; it's just so on all farms."

"Yes, I guess it is," said she. "Father was a carpenter, and I've always lived here; but we have people who are farmers, and I know how it is with them."

"Why, when I think of it now it makes me crawl! To think of getting up in the morning before daylight, and going out to the barn to do chores, to get ready to go into the field to work! Working, wasting y'r life on dirt. Goin' round and round in a circle, and never getting out."

"It's just the same for us women," she corroborated. "Think of us going around the house day after day, and doing just the same things over an' over, year after year! That's the whole of most women's lives. Dish-washing almost drives me crazy."

"I know it," said Albert; "but a fellow has t' do it. If his folks are workin' hard, why, of course he can't lay around and study. They're not to blame. I don't know that anybody's to blame."

"No, I don't; but it makes me sad to see mother going around as she does, day after day. She won't let me do as much as I would." The girl looked at her slender hands. "You see, I'm not very strong. It makes my heart ache to see her going around in that quiet, patient way; she's so good."

"I know, I know! I've felt just like that about my mother and father, too."

There was a long pause, full of deep feeling, and then the girl continued in a low, hesitating voice:

"Mother's had an awful hard time since father died. We had to go to keeping boarders, which was hard—very hard for mother." The boy felt a sympathetic lump in his throat as the girl went on again: "But she doesn't complain, and she didn't want me to come home from school; but of course I couldn't do anything else."

It didn't occur to either of them that any other course was open, nor that there was any heroism or self-sacrifice in the act; it was simply *right*.

"Well, I'm not going to drudge all my life," said the boy at last. "I know it's kind o' selfish, but I can't live on a farm; it 'u'd kill me in a year. I've made up my mind to study law and enter the bar. Lawyers manage to get hold of enough to live on decently, and that's more than you can say of the farmers. And they live in town, where something is going on once in a while, anyway."

In the pause which followed, footsteps were heard on the walk outside, and the girl sprang up with a beautiful blush.

"My stars! I didn't think—I forgot—I must go."

Hartley burst into the room shortly after she left it, in his usual breeze.

"Hul-*lo*! Still at the Latin, hey?"

"Yes," said Bert, with ease. "How goes it?"

"Oh, I'm whooping 'er up! I'm getting started in great shape. Been up to the courthouse and roped in three of the county officials. In these small towns the big man is the politician or the clergyman. I've nailed the politicians through the ear; now you must go for the ministers to head the list—that's your lay-out."

"How'm I t' do it?" said Bert, in an anxious tone. "I can't sell books if they don't want 'em."

"Yes, yeh can. That's the trade. Offer a big discount. Say full calf, two fifty; morocco, two ninety. Regular discount to the clergy, ye know. Oh, they're on to that little racket—no trouble. If you can get a few of these leaders of the flock, the rest will follow like lambs to the slaughter. Tra-la-la—who-o-o-*ish*, whish!"

Albert laughed at Hartley as he plunged his face into the ice-cold water, puffing and wheezing.

"Jeemimy Crickets! but ain't that water cold! I worked Rock River this way last month, and made a boomin' success. If you take hold here in the—"

"Oh, I'm all ready to do anything that is needed, short of being kicked out."

"No danger of that if you're a real book agent. It's the snide that gets kicked. You've got t' have some savvy in this, just like any other business." He stopped in his dressing to say, "We've struck a great boarding place, hey?"

"Looks like it."

"I begin t' cotton to the old lady a'ready. Good 'eal like mother used t' be 'fore she broke down. Didn't the old lady have a time of it raisin' me? Phewee! Patient! Job wasn't a patchin'. But the test is goin' t' come on the biscuit; if her biscuit comes up t' mother's I'm hern till death."

He broke off to comb his hair, a very nice bit of work in his case.

II

There was no discernible reason why the little town should have been called Tyre, and yet its name was as characteristically American as its architecture. It had the usual main street lined with low brick or wooden stores—a street which developed into a road running back up a wide, sandy valley away from the river. Being a county town, it had a courthouse in a yard near the center of the town, and a big summer hotel. The valley was peculiarly picturesque. Curiously shaped and oddly distributed hills rose out of the valley sand abruptly, forming a sort of amphitheater in which the village lay. These square-topped hills rose to a common level, showing that they were not the result of an upheaval, but were the remains of the original stratification left standing after the vast scooping action of the post-glacial floods.

The abrupt cliffs and lone huge pillars and peaks rising out of tamarack swamps here and there showed the original layers of rock unmoved. They looked like ruined walls of castles ancient as hills, on whose massive tops time had sown sturdy oaks and cedars. They lent a distinct air of romance to the valley at all times; but when in summer vines clambered over their rugged sides and underbrush softened their broken lines, it was not at all difficult to imagine them the remains of an unrecorded, very warlike people.

Even now, in winter, with yellow-brown and green cedars standing starkly upon their summits, the hickories and small ashes blue-black with their masses of fine bare limbs meshed against the snow, these towers had a distinct charm. The weather was glorious winter, and in the early morning when the trees glistened with frost, or at evening when the white light of the sun was softened and violet shadows lay along the snow, the whole valley was a delight to the eye, full of distinct and lasting charm, part of the beautiful and strange Mississippi River scenery.

In the campaign which Hartley began Albert did his best, and his best was done unconsciously, for the charm of his manner (all unknown to himself) was the most potent factor in securing consideration.

"I'm not a book agent," he said to one of the clergymen to whom he first appealed; "I'm a student trying to sell a good book and make a little money to help me to complete my course at the university."

He did not go to the back door, but walked up to the front, asked to see the minister, and placed his case at once before him with a smiling candor and a leisurely utterance quite the opposites of the brazen timidity and rapid, parrot-like tone of the professional. He secured three clergymen of the place to head his list, much to the delight and admiration of Hartley.

"Good! Now corral the alumni of the place. Work the fraternal racket to the bitter end. Oh, say! there's a sociable to-morrow night; I guess we'd better go, hadn't we?"

"Go alone?"

"Alone? No! Take some girls. I'm going to take neighbor Picket's daughter; she's homely as a hedge fence, but I'll take her—great scheme!"

"Hartley, you're an infernal fraud!"

"Nothing of the kind—I'm business," ended Hartley, with a laugh.

After supper the following day, as Albert was still lingering at the table with the girls and Mrs. Welsh, he thought of the sociable, and said on the impulse:

"Are you going to the sociable?"

"No; I guess not."

"Would you go if I asked you?"

"Try me and see!" answered the girl, with a laugh, her color rising.

"All right. Miss Welsh, will you attend the festivity of the evening under my guidance and protection?"

"Yes, thank you."

"I'll be ready before you are."

"No doubt; I've got to wash the dishes."

"I'll wash the dishes; you go get ready," said the self-regardless mother.

Albert felt that he had one of the loveliest girls in the room as he led Maud down the floor of the vestry of the church, filled with laughing young people moving about or seated at the long tables. Maud's cheeks were full of delicate color and her eyes shone with maidenly delight as they took seats at the table to sip a little coffee and nibble a bit of cake.

"I suppose they *must* have my fifteen cents some way," said Albert, in a low voice, "and I guess we'd better sit down."

Maud introduced him to a number of young people who had

Hamlin Garland

been students at the university. They received him cordially, and in a very short time he was enjoying himself very well indeed. He was reminded rather disagreeably of his office, however, by seeing Hartley surrounded by a laughing crowd of the more frolicsome young people. He winked at Albert, as much as to say, "Good stroke of business."

The evening passed away with songs, games, and recitations, and it was nearly eleven o'clock when the young people began to wander off toward home in pairs. Albert and Maud were among the first of the young folks to bid the rest good night.

The night was clear and cold, but perfectly still, and the young people, arm in arm, walked slowly homeward under the bare maples, in delicious companionship. Albert held her arm close to his side.

"Are you cold?" he asked in a low voice.

"No, thank you; the night is lovely," she replied; then added with a sigh, "I don't like sociables so well as I used to—they tire me out."

"We stayed too long."

"It wasn't that; I'm getting so they seem kind o' silly."

"Well, I feel a little that way myself," he confessed.

"But there is so little to see here in Tyre at any time—no music, no theaters. I like theaters, don't you?"

"I can't go half enough."

"But nothing worth seeing ever comes into these little

towns—and then we're all so poor, anyway."

The lamp, turned low, was emitting a terrible odor as they entered the sitting room.

"My goodness! it's almost twelve o'clock. Good night." She held out her hand.

"Good night," he said, taking it, and giving it a cordial pressure which she remembered long.

"Good night," she repeated softly, going up the stairs.

Hartley came in a few moments later, and found Bert sitting thoughtfully by the fire, with his coat and shoes off, evidently in deep abstraction.

"Well, I got away at last—much as ever. Great scheme, that sociable, eh? I saw your little girl introducing you right and left."

"Say, Hartley, I wish you'd leave her out of this thing; I don't like the way you speak of her when—"

"Phew! You don't? Oh, all right! I'm mum as an oyster—only keep it up! Get in all the church sociables, and all that; there's nothing like it."

Hartley soon had canvassers out along the country roads, and was working every house in town. The campaign promised to lengthen into a month, perhaps longer. Albert especially became a great favorite. Every one declared there had never been such book agents in the town: such gentlemanly fellows, they didn't press anybody to buy; they didn't rush about and "poke their noses where they were not wanted." They were more like merchants with books to sell. The only person who failed to see the attraction in them was Ed Brann, who was popularly supposed to be engaged to Maud. He grew daily more sullen and repellent, toward Albert noticeably so.

One evening about six, after coming in from a long walk about town, Albert entered his room without lighting his lamp, lay down on the bed, and fell asleep. He had been out late the night before with Maud at a party, and slumber came almost instantly.

Maud came in shortly, hearing no response to her knock, and after hanging some towels on the rack went out without seeing the sleeper. In the sitting room she met Ed Brann. He was a stalwart young man with curling black hair, and a heavy face at its best, but set and sullen now. His first words held a menace:

"Say, Maud, I want t' talk to you."

"Very well; what is it, Ed?" replied the girl quietly.

"I want to know how often you're going to be out till twelve o'clock with this book agent?"

Perhaps it was the derisive inflection on "book agent" that woke Albert. Brann's tone was brutal—more brutal even than his words, and the girl turned pale and her breath quickened.

"Why, Ed, what's the matter?"

"Matter is just this: you ain't got any business goin' around with that feller with my ring on your finger, that's all." He ended with an unmistakable threat in his voice.

"Very well," said the girl, after a pause, curiously quiet;

"then I won't; here's your ring."

The man's bluster disappeared instantly. Bert could tell by the change in his voice, which was incredibly great, as he pleaded:

"Oh, don't do that, Maud; I didn't mean to say that; I was mad—I'm sorry."

"I'm *glad* you did it *now*, so I can know you. Take your ring, Ed; I never'll wear it again."

Albert had heard all this, but he did not know how the girl looked as she faced the man. In the silence which followed she looked him in the face, and scornfully passed him and went out into the kitchen. He did not return at supper.

Young people of this sort are not self-analysts, and Maud did not examine closely into causes. She was astonished to find herself more indignant than grieved. She broke into an angry wail as she went to her mother's bosom:

"Mother! mother!"

"Why, what's the matter, Maudie? Tell me. There, there! don't cry, pet! Who's been hurtin' my poor little bird?"

"Ed has; he said—he said—"

"There, there! poor child! Have you been quarreling? Never mind; it'll come out all right."

"No, it won't—not the way you mean," the girl cried, lifting her head; "I've given him back his ring, and I'll never wear it again."

The mother could not understand with what wounding brutality the man's tone had fallen upon the girl's spirit, and Maud felt in some way as if she could not explain sufficiently to justify herself. Mrs. Welsh consoled herself with the idea that it was only a lovers' quarrel—one of the little jars sure to come when two natures are settling together—and that all would be mended in a day or two.

But there was a peculiar set look on the girl's face that promised little for Brann. Albert, being no more of a self-analyst than Maud, simply said, "Served him right," and dwelt no more upon it for the time.

At supper, however, he was extravagantly gay, and to himself unaccountably so. He joked Troutt till Maud begged him to stop, and after the rest had gone he remained seated at the table, enjoying the indignant color in her face and the flash of her infrequent smile, which it was such a pleasure to provoke. He volunteered to help wash the dishes.

"Thank you, but I'm afraid you'd be more bother than help," she replied.

"Thank *you*, but you don't know me. I ain't so green as I look, by no manner o' means. I've been doing my own housekeeping for four terms."

"I know all about that," laughed the girl. "You young men rooming do precious little cooking and no dish-washing at all."

"That's a base calumny! I made it a point to wash every dish in the house, except the spider, once a week; had a regular cleaning-up day."

"And about the spider?"

"I wiped that out nicely with a newspaper every time I wanted to use it."

"Oh, horrors!—Mother, listen to that!"

"Why, what more could you ask? You wouldn't have me wipe it *six* times a day, would you?"

"I wonder it didn't poison you," commented Mrs. Welsh.

"Takes more'n that to poison a student," laughed Albert, as he went out.

The next afternoon he came bursting into the kitchen, where Maud stood with her sleeves rolled up, deep in the dish pan, while Stella stood wiping the dishes handed to her.

"Don't you want a sleigh ride?" he asked, boyishly eager.

She looked up with shining eyes.

"Oh, wouldn't I!—Can you get along, mother?"

"Certainly, child; the air'll do you good."

"W'y, Maud!" said the little girl, "you said you didn't want to when Ed—"

Mrs. Welsh silenced her, and said:

"Run right along, dear; it's just the nicest time o' day. Are there many teams out?"

"They're just beginning t' come out," said Albert. "I'll have a cutter around here in about two jiffies; be on hand, sure."

Troutt was standing in the sunny doorway of his stable when the young fellow dashed up to him.

"Hullo, Uncle Troutt! Harness the fastest nag into your swellest outfit instanter."

"Aha! Goin' t' take y'r girl out, hey?"

"Yes; and I want 'o do it in style."

"I guess ol' Dan's the idee, if you can drive him; he's a ring-tailed snorter."

"Fast?"

"Nope; but safe. Gentle as a kitten and as knowin' as a fox. Drive him with one hand—left hand," the old man chuckled.

"Troutt, you're an insinuating old insinuator, and I'll—"

Troutt laughed till his long faded beard flapped up and down and quivered with the stress of his enjoyment of his joke. He ended by hitching a vicious-looking sorrel to a gay, duck-bellied cutter, saying as he gave up the reins:

"Now, be keerful; Dan's foxy; he's all right when he sees you've got the reins, but don't drop 'em."

"Don't you worry about me; I grew up with horses," said the over-confident youth, leaping into the sleigh and gathering up the lines. "Stand aside, my lord, and let the cortege pass. Hoop-la!"

The brute gave a tearing lunge, and was out of the doorway like a shot before the old man could utter a word. Albert thrilled with pleasure as he felt the reins stiffen in his hands, while the traces swung slack beside the thills.

"If he keeps this up he'll do," he thought.

As he turned up at the gate Maud came gayly down the path, muffled to the eyes.

"Oh, what a nice cutter! But the horse—is he gentle?" she asked, as she climbed in.

"As a cow," Albert replied.—"Git out o' this, Bones!"

The main street was already full of teams, wood sleighs, bob-sleighs filled with children, and here and there a man in a light cutter alone, out for a race. Laughter was on the air, and the jingle-jangle of bells. The sun was dazzling in its brightness, and the gay wraps and scarfs lighted up the street with flecks of color. Loafers on the sidewalks fired a fusillade of words at the teams as they passed:

"Go it, Bones!"

"'Let 'er *go*, Gallagher!'"

"Ain't she a daisy!"

But what cared the drivers? If the shouts were insolent they laid them to envy, and if they were pleasant they smiled in reply.

Albert and Maud had made two easy turns up and down the street, when a man driving a span of large black-hawk horses dashed up a side street and whirled in just before them. The man was a superb driver, and sat with the reins held carelessly but securely in his left hand, guiding the team more by his voice than by the bit. He sat leaning forward with his head held down in a peculiar and sinister fashion.

"*Hel*-lo!" cried Bert; "that looks like Brann."

"It is," said Maud.

"Cracky! that's a fine team—Black Hawks, both of them. I wonder if ol' sorrel can pass 'em?"

"Oh, please don't try," pleaded the girl.

"Why not?"

"Because—because I'm afraid."

"Afraid of what?"

"Afraid something'll happen."

"Something *is* goin' t' happen; I'm goin' t' pass him if old Bones has got any *git* to him."

"It'll make him mad."

"Who mad? Brann?"

"Yes."

"Well, s'pose it does, who cares?"

The teams moved along at an easy pace. Some one called to Brann:

"They're on y'r trail, Ed."

There was something peculiar in the tone, and Brann looked

behind for the first time, and saw them. He swore through his teeth, and turned about. He looked dogged and sullen, with his bent shoulders and his chin thrust down.

There were a dozen similar rigs moving up or down the street, and greetings passed from sleigh to sleigh. Everybody except Brann welcomed Albert with sincere pleasure, and exchanged rustic jokes with him. As they slowed up at the upper end of the street and began to turn, a man on the sidewalk said confidentially:

"Say, cap', if you handle that old rack-o'-bones just right, he'll distance anything on this road. When you want him to do his best let him have the rein; don't pull a pound. I used to own 'im—I know 'im."

The old sorrel came round "gauming," his ugly head thrown up, his great red mouth open, his ears back. Brann and the young doctor of the place were turning together a little farther up the street. The blacks, superbly obedient to their driver, came down with flying hoofs, their great glossy breasts flecked with foam from their champing jaws.

"Come on, fellers!" yelled Brann, insultingly, as he came down past the doctor, and seemed about to pass Albert and Maud. There was hate in the glare of his eyes.

But he did not pass. The old sorrel seemed to lengthen; to the spectators his nose appeared to be glued to the glossy side of Brann's off black.

"See them blacks trot!" shouted Albert, in ungrammatical enthusiasm.

"See that old sorrel shake himself!" yelled the loafers.

The doctor came tearing down with a spirited bay, a magnificent stepper. As he drew along so that Bert could catch a glimpse of the mare's neck, he thrilled with delight. There was the thoroughbred's lacing of veins; the proud fling of her knees and the swell of her neck showed that she was far from doing her best. There was a wild light in her eyes.

These were the fast teams of the town. All interest was centered in them.

"Clear the track!" yelled the loafers.

"The doc's good f'r 'em."

"If she don't break."

Albert was pulling at the sorrel heavily, absorbed in seeing, as well as he could for the flung snowballs, the doctor's mare draw slowly, foot by foot, past the blacks. Suddenly Brann gave a shrill yell and stood up in his sleigh. The gallant little bay broke and fell behind; Brann gave a loud laugh; the blacks trotted on, their splendid pace unchanged.

"Let the sorrel out!" yelled somebody.

"Let him loose!" yelled Troutt on the corner, quivering with excitement. "Let him go!"

Albert remembered what the fellow had said; he let the reins loose. The old sorrel's teeth came together with a snap; his head lowered and his tail rose; he shot abreast of the blacks. Brann yelled:

"Sam—Saul, *git*!"

"See them trot!" shouted Bert, lost in admiration; but Maud, frightened into silence, had covered her head with the robe to escape the blinding cloud of flying snow. The sorrel drew steadily ahead; he was passing when Brann turned.

"Durn y'r old horse!" he yelled through his shut teeth, and laid the whip across the sorrel's hips. The blacks broke wildly, but, strange to say, the old sorrel increased his speed. Again Brann struck at him, but missed him, and the stroke fell on Bert's outstretched wrists. He turned to see what Brann meant by it; he did not see that the blacks were crowding him to the gutter; his hands felt numb.

"Look *out*, there!"

Before he could turn to look, the cutter seemed to be blown up by a bomb, and he rose in the air like a vaulter; he saw the traces part, he felt the reins slip through his hands, and that was all; he seemed to fall an immeasurable depth into a black abyss.... The next that he knew was a curious soft murmur of voices, out of which a sweet, agonized girl-voice broke, familiar but unrecognized:

"Oh, where's the doctor! He's dead—oh, he's dead! *Can't* you hurry?"

Next came a quick, authoritative voice, still far away, and a hush followed it; then an imperative order:

"Stand out o' the way! What do you think you can do by crowding on top of him?"

"Stand back! stand back!" other voices called.

Then he felt something cold on his head: they were taking his cap off and putting snow on his head; then the doctor (he knew him now) said:

Hamlin Garland

"Let me take him!"

"Oh, can't I do something?" said the sweet voice.

"No—nothing."

Then there came a strange fullness in his head. Shadows lighted by dull red flashes passed before his eyes; he wondered, in a slow, dull way, if he were dying. Then this changed: a dull, throbbing ache came into his head, and as this grew the noise of voices grew more distinct and he could hear sobbing. Then the dull, rhythmic red flashes passed slowly away from his eyes, and he opened his lids, but the glare of the sunlight struck them shut again; he saw only Maud's face, agonized, white, and wet with tears, looking down into his. He felt the doctor's hands winding bandages about his head, and he felt a crawling stream of blood behind his ear, getting as cold as ice as it sank under his collar.

They raised him a little more, and he opened his eyes on the circle of hushed and excited men thronging about him. He saw Brann, with wild, scared face, standing in his cutter and peering over the heads of the crowd.

"How do you feel now?" asked the doctor.

"Can you hear us? Albert, do you know me?" called the girl.

His lips moved stiffly, but he smiled a little, and at length whispered slowly, "Yes; I guess—I'm all—right."

"Put him into my cutter; Maud, get in here, too," the doctor commanded, with all the authority of a physician in a small village. The crowd opened, and silenced its muttered comments as the doctor and Troutt helped the wounded man into the sleigh. The pain in his head grew worse, but Albert's perception of things grew in proportion; he closed his eyes to the sun, but in the shadow of Maud's breast opened them again and looked up at her. He felt a vague, childlike pleasure in knowing she was holding him in her arms; he felt the sleigh moving; he thought of his mother, and how it would frighten her if she knew.

The doctor was driving the horse and walking beside the sleigh, and the people were accosting him. Albert could catch their words now and then, and the reply:

"No; he isn't killed, nor anything near it; he's stunned, that's all; he isn't bleeding now. No; he'll be all right in a day or two."

"Hello!" said a breathless, hearty voice, "what the deuce y' been doing with my pardner? Bert, old fellow, are you there?" Hartley asked, clinging to the edge of the moving cutter, and peering into his friend's face. Albert smiled.

"I'm here—what there is left of me," he replied faintly.

"Glory! how'd it happen?" he asked of the girl.

"I don't know—I couldn't see—we ran into a culvert," replied Maud.

"Weren't you hurt?"

"Not a bit. I stayed in the cutter."

Albert felt a steady return of waves of pain, but did not know that they were waves of returning life. He groaned, and tried to rise. The girl gently but firmly restrained him. Hartley was walking beside the doctor, talking loudly. "It was a devilish thing to do; the scoundrel ought 'o be jugged!"

Albert groaned, and tried to rise again. "I'm bleeding yet; I'm soaking you!"

The girl shuddered, but remained firm.

"No; we're 'most home."

She felt no shame, but a certain exaltation, as she looked into the curious faces she saw in groups on the sidewalk. The boys who ran alongside wore in their faces a look of awe, for they imagined themselves in the presence of death.

Maud gazed unrecognizingly upon her nearest girl friends. They seemed something alien in that moment; and they, gazing upon her white face and unrecognizing eyes, spoke in awed whispers.

At the gate the crowd gathered and waited with deepest interest, with a sort of shuddering pleasure. It was all a strange, unusual, inthralling romance to them. The dazzling sunshine added to the wonder of it all.

"Ed Brann done it."

"How?" asked several.

"With the butt end of his whip."

"That's a lie! His team ran into Lohr's rig."

"Not much; Ed crowded him into the ditch."

"What fer?"

"'Cause Bert cut him out with Maud."

"Come, get out of the way! Don't stand there gabbing," yelled Hartley, as he took Albert in his arms and, together with the doctor, lifted him out of the sleigh.

"Goodness sakes alive! Ain't it terrible! How is he?" asked an old lady, peering at him as he passed.

On the porch stood Mrs. Welsh, supported by Ed Brann.

"She's all right, I tell you. He ain't hurt much, either; just stunned a little, that's all."

"Maud! child!" cried the mother, as Maud appeared out of the crowd, followed by a bevy of girls.

"Mother, *I'm* all right!" she said as gayly as she could, running into the trembling arms outstretched toward her; "but, oh, poor Albert!"

After they disappeared into the house the crowd dispersed. Brann went off by way of the alley; he was not prepared to meet their questions; but he met his brother and several others in his store.

"Now, what in—you been up to?" was the fraternal greeting.

"Nothing."

"Welting a man on the head with a whip-stock ain't anything, hey?"

"I didn't touch him. We was racing, and he run into the culvert."

"Hank says he saw you strike—"

"He lies! I was strikin' the horse to make him break."

"Oh, yeh was!" sneered the older man. "Well, I hope you understand that this'll ruin us in this town. If you didn't strike him, they'll say you run him into the culvert, 'n' every man, woman, 'n' child'll be down on you, and *me* f'r bein' related to you. They all know how you feel towards him for cuttin' you out with Maud Welsh."

"Oh, don't bear down on him too hard, Joe. He didn't mean t' do any harm," said Troutt, who had followed Ed down to the store. "I guess the young feller'll come out all right. Just go kind o' easy till we see how he comes out. If he dies, why, it'll haf t' be looked into."

Ed turned pale and swallowed hastily. "If he should die!" He would be a murderer; he knew that hate was in his heart. He shivered again as he remembered the man's white face with the bright red stream flowing down behind his ear and over his cheek. It almost seemed to him that he *had* struck him, so close had the accident followed upon the fall of his whip.

III

Albert sank into a feverish sleep that night, with a vague perception of four figures in the room—Maud, her mother, Hartley, and the young doctor. When he awoke fully in the morning his head felt prodigiously hot and heavy.

It was early dawn, and the lamp was burning brightly. Outside, a man's feet could be heard on the squealing snow—a sound which told how still and cold it was. A team passed with a jingle of bells.

Albert raised his head and looked about. Hartley was lying on the sofa, rolled up in his overcoat and some extra quilts. He had lain down at last, worn with watching. Albert felt a little weak, and fell back on his pillow, thinking about the strange night he had passed—a night more filled with strange happenings than the afternoon.

His sleep had been broken by the most vivid and exciting dreams, and through these visions had moved the figures of Hartley, the doctor, and Maud and her mother. He had a confused idea of the night, but a very clear idea of the afternoon. He could see the sidewalks lined with faces, the sun shining on the snow, the old sorrel's side-flung head and open mouth; the sleigh rose under him again, and he felt the reins burn through his hands.

As the light grew in the room his mind cleared, and he began to feel quite like himself again. He lifted his muscular arm and opened and shut his hand, saying aloud in his old boyish manner:

"I guess I'm all here."

"What's that?" called Hartley, rolling out of bed. "Did you ask for anything?"

"No—yes; gimme some water, Jim; my mouth is dry as a powder mill."

"How yeh feelin', anyway, pardner?" said Hartley, as he brought the water.

"First rate, Jim; I guess I'll be all right."

"Well, I guess you'd better keep quiet."

Albert rose partly, assisted by his friend, and drank from the glass a moment; then fell back on his pillow.

"I don't feel s' well when I sit up."

"Well, don't, then; stay right there where you are. Oh-um!" gaped Hartley, stretching himself; "it's about time f'r breakfast, I guess. Want y'r hands washed and y'r hair combed?"

"I guess I ain't reduced to *that* yet."

"Well, I guess y' *be*, old man. Now keep *quiet*, or have I got t' make yeh?" he asked in a threatening tone which made Albert smile. He wondered if Hartley hadn't been sitting up most of the night; but if he had, he showed little effect of it, for he began to sing a comic song as he pulled on his boots.

He threw on his coat next, and went out into the kitchen, returning soon with some hot water, with which he began to bathe the wounded boy's face and hands as tenderly as a woman.

"There; now I guess you're in shape f'r grub—feel any like

grub?—Come in," he called in answer to a knock on the door.

Mrs. Welsh entered.

"How is he?" she whispered anxiously.

"Oh, I'm all right," cried Albert. "Bring me a plate of pancakes, quick!"

Mrs. Welsh turned to Hartley with a startled expression, but Hartley's grin assured her.

"I'm glad to find you so much better," she said, going to his bedside. "I've hardly slep', I was so much worried about you."

It was very sweet to feel her fingers in his hair, as his mother would have caressed him.

"I guess I hadn't better take off the bandages till the doctor comes, if you're comfortable.—Your breakfast is ready, Mr. Hartley, and I'll bring something for Albert."

Another knock a few minutes later, and Maud entered with a platter, followed closely by her mother, who carried some tea and milk.

Maud came forward timidly, but when he turned his eyes on her and said in a cheery voice, "Good morning, Miss Welsh!" she flamed out in rosy color and recoiled. She had expected to see him pale, dull-eyed, and with a weak voice, but there was little to indicate invalidism in his firm greeting. She gave place to Mrs. Welsh, who prepared his breakfast. She was smitten dumb by this turn of affairs; she hardly dared look at him as he sat propped up in bed. The crimson trimming on his shirt-front seemed like streams of blood; his head, swathed in bandages, made her shudder. But aside from these few suggestions of wounding, there was little of the horror of the previous day left. He did not look so pale and worn as the girl herself.

However, though he was feeling absurdly well, there was a good deal of bravado in his tone and manner, for he ate but little, and soon sank back on the bed.

"I feel better when my head is low," he explained in a faint voice.

"Can't I do something?" asked the girl, her courage reviving as she saw how ill and faint he really was. His eyes were closed and he looked the invalid now.

"I guess you better write to his folks."

"No; don't do that," he said, opening his eyes; "it will only do them harm an' me no good. I'll be all right in a few days. You needn't waste your time on me; Hartley'll wait on me."

"Mr. Lohr, how can you say such cruel—"

"Don't mind him now," said Mrs. Welsh. "I'm his mother now, and he's goin' to do just as I tell him to—ain't you, Albert?"

He dropped his eyelids in assent, and went off in a doze. It was all very pleasant to be thus treated. Hartley was devotion itself, and the doctor removed his bandages with the care and deliberation of a man with a moderate practice; besides, he considered Albert a personal friend.

Hartley, after the doctor had gone, said with some hesitation:

"Well, now, pard, I *ought* to go out and see a couple o' fellows I promised t' meet this morning."

"All right, Jim; all right. You go right ahead on business; I'm goin' t' sleep, anyway, and I'll be all right in a day or two."

"Well, I will; but I'll run in every hour 'r two and see if you don't want something. You're in good hands, anyway, when I'm gone."

"Won't you read to me?" pleaded Albert in the afternoon, when Maud came in with her mother to brush up the room. "It's getting rather slow business layin' here like this. Course I can't ask Jim to stay and read all the time, and he's a bad reader, anyway; won't you?"

"Shall I, mother?"

"Why, of course, Maud!"

So Maud got a book, and sat down over by the stove, quite distant from the bed, and read to him from "The Lady of the Lake," while the mother, like a piece of tireless machinery, moved about the house at the never-ending succession of petty drudgeries which wear the heart and soul out of so many wives and mothers, making life to them a pilgrimage from stove to pantry, from pantry to cellar, and from cellar to garret—a life that deadens and destroys, coarsens and narrows, till the flesh and bones are warped to the expression of the wronged and cheated soul.

Albert's selfishness was in a way excusable. He enjoyed beyond measure the sound of the girl's soft voice and the sight of her graceful head bent over the page. He lay, looking and listening dreamily, till the voice and the sunlit head were lost in his deep, sweet sleep.

The girl sat with closed book, looking at his face as he slept. It was a curious study to her, a young man—*this* young man, asleep. His brown lashes lay on his cheek; his facial lines were as placid as a child's. As she looked she gained courage to go over softly and peer down on him. How boyish he seemed! How little to be feared! How innocent, after all!

As she studied him she thought of him the day before, with closed eyes, a ghastly stream of blood flowing down and soaking her dress. She shuddered. His hands, clean and strong and white, lay out on the coverlet, loose and open, the fingers fallen into graceful lines. Abruptly, a boy outside gave a shout, and she leaped away with a sudden spring that left her pale and breathless. As she paused in the door and looked back at the undisturbed sleeper, she smiled, and the pink came back into her thin face.

Albert's superb young blood began to assert itself, and on the afternoon of the second day he was able to sit in his rocking chair before the fire and read a little, though he professed that his eyes were not strong, in order that Maud should read for him. This she did as often as she could leave her other work, which was "not half often enough," the invalid grumbled.

"More than you deserve," she found courage to say.

Hartley let nothing interfere with the book business, and the popular sympathy for Albert he coined into dollars remorselessly.

"You take it easy," he kept saying to his partner; "don't you worry—your pay goes on just the same. You're doing well right where you are. By jinks! biggest piece o' luck," he went on, half in earnest. "Why, I can't turn around without taking an order—fact! Turned in a book on the livery bill—that's all right. We'll make a clear hundred dollars out o' that little bump o' yours."

"Little bump! Say, now, that's—"

"Keep it up—put it on! Don't get up in a hurry. I don't need you to canvass, and I guess you enjoy this 'bout as well." He ended with a sly wink and cough.

Yes; the convalescence was delicious; afterward it grew to be one of the sweetest weeks of his life. Maud reading to him, bringing his food, and singing for him—yes; all that marred it was the stream of people who came to inquire how he was getting along. The sympathy was largely genuine, as Hartley could attest, but it bored the invalid. He had rather be left in quiet with Walter Scott and Maud, the drone of the long descriptive passages being a sure soporific.

He did not say, as an older person might, that she was not to be held accountable for what she did under the stress and tumult of that day; but he unconsciously did so regard her actions, led to do so by the changed conditions. In the light of common day it was hurrying to be a dream.

At the end of a week he was quite himself again, though he still had difficulty in wearing his hat. It was not till the second Sunday after the accident that he appeared in the dining room for the first time, with a large traveling cap concealing the suggestive bandages. He looked pale and thin, but his eyes danced with joy.

Maud's eyes dilated with instant solicitude. The rest sprang up in surprise, with shouts of delight, as hearty as brethren.

"Ginger! I'm glad t' see yeh!" said Troutt, so sincerely that he looked almost winning to the boy. The rest crowded around, shaking hands.

"Oh, I'm on deck again."

Ed Brann came in a moment later with his brother, and there was a significant little pause—a pause which grew painful till Albert turned and saw Brann, and called out:

"Hello, Ed! How are you? Didn't know you were here."

As he held out his hand, Brann, his face purple with shame and embarrassment, lumbered heavily across the room and took it, muttering some poor apology.

"Hope y' don't blame me."

"Of course not—fortunes o' war. Nobody to blame; just my carelessness.—Yes; I'll take turkey," he said to Maud, as he sank into the seat of honor at the head of the table.

Then the rest laughed and took seats, but Brann remained standing near Albert's chair. He had not finished yet.

"I'm mighty glad yeh don't lay it up against me, Lohr; an' I want 'o say the doctor's bill is all right; you un'erstand, it's *all right*."

Albert looked at him a moment in surprise. He knew this, coming from a man like Brann, meant more than a thousand prayers from a ready apologist; it was a terrible victory, and he made it as easy for his rival as possible.

"Oh, all right, Ed; only I'd calculated to cheat him out o' part of it—that is, turn in a couple o' Blaine's 'Twenty Years' on the bill."

Hartley roared, and the rest joined in, but not even Albert perceived all that it meant. It meant that the young savage had surrendered his claim in favor of the man he had all but killed. The struggle had been prodigious, but he had snatched victory out of defeat; his better nature had conquered.

No one ever gave him credit for it; and when he went West in the spring, people said his love for Maud had been superficial. In truth, he had loved the girl as sincerely as he had hated his rival. That he could rise out of the barbaric in his love and hate was heroic.

When Albert went to ride again, it was on melting snow, with the slowest horse Troutt had. Maud was happier than she had been since she left school, and fuller of color and singing. She dared not let a golden moment pass now without hearing it ring full, and she did not dare to think how short this day of happiness might be.

IV

At the end of the fifth week there was a suspicion of spring in the wind as it swept the southern exposure of the valley. February was drawing to a close, and there was more than a suggestion of spring in the rapidly melting snow which still lay on the hills and under the cedars and tamaracks in the swamps. Patches of green grass, appearing on the sunny side of the road where the snow had melted, led to predictions of spring from the loafers beginning to sun themselves on the salt-barrels and shoe-boxes outside the stores.

A group sitting about the blacksmith shop were talking it.

"It's an early seedin'—now mark my words," said Troutt, as he threw his knife into the soft ground at his feet. "The sun is crossing the line earlier this spring than it did last."

"Yes; an' I heard a crow to-day makin' that kind of a—a spring noise that kind o'—I d' know what—kind o' goes all through a feller."

"And there's Uncle Sweeney, an' that settles it; spring's comin' sure!" said Troutt, pointing at an old man much bent, hobbling down the street like a symbolic figure of the old year.

"When *he* gits out the frogs ain't fur behind."

"We'll be gittin' on to the ground by next Monday," said Sam Dingley to a crowd who were seated on the newly painted harrows and seeders which "Svend & Johnson" had got out ready for the spring trade. "Svend & Johnson's Agricultural Implement Depot" was on the north side of the street, and on a spring day the yard was one of the pleasantest loafing places that could be imagined, especially if one wished company.

Albert wished to be alone. Something in the touch and tone of this spring afternoon made him restless and full of strange thoughts. He took his way out along the road which followed the river bank, and in the outskirts of the village threw himself down on a bank of grass which the snows had protected, and which had already a tinge of green because of its wealth of sun.

The willows had thrown out their tiny light green flags, though their roots were under the ice, and some of the hardwood twigs were tinged with red. There was a faint, peculiar but powerful odor of uncovered earth in the air, and the touch of the wind was like a caress from a moist magnetic hand.

The boy absorbed the light and heat of the sun as some wild thing might, his hat over his face, his hands folded on his breast; he lay as still as a statue. He did not listen at first, he only felt; but at length he rose on his elbow and listened. The ice cracked and fell along the bank with a long, hollow, booming crash; a crow cawed, and a jay answered it from the willows below. A flight of sparrows passed, twittering innumerably. The boy shuddered with a strange, wistful longing and a realization of the flight of time.

He could have wept, he could have sung; he only shuddered and lay silent under the stress of that strange, sweet passion that quickened his heart, deepened his eyes, and made his breath come and go with a quivering sound. Across the dazzling blue arch of the sky the crow flapped, sending down his prophetic, jubilant note; the wind, as soft and sweet as April, stirred in his hair; the hills, deep in their dusky blue, seemed miles away; and the voices of the care-free skaters

Hamlin Garland

on the melting ice of the river below came to the ear subdued to a unity with the scene.

Suddenly a fear seized upon the boy—a horror! Life, life was passing! Life that can be lived only once, and lost, is lost forever! Life, that fatal gift of the Invisible Powers to man— a path, with youth and joy and hope at its eastern gate, and despair, regret, and death at its low western portal!

The boy caught a glimpse of his real significance—a gnat, a speck in the sun: a boy facing the millions of great and wise and wealthy. He leaped up, clasping his hands.

"Oh, I *must* work! I mustn't stay here; I must get back to my studies. Life is slipping by me, and I am doing nothing, being nothing!"

His face, as pale as death, absolutely shone with his passionate resolution, and his hands were clinched in a silent, inarticulate desire.

But on his way back he met the jocund party of skaters going home from the river, and with the easy shift and change of youth joined in their ringing laughter. The weird power of the wind's voice was gone, and he was the unthinking boy again; but the problem was only put off, not solved.

He had a suspicion of it one night when Hartley said: "Well, pardner, we're getting 'most ready to pull out. Some way I always get restless when these warm days begin. Want 'o be moving some way."

This was as sentimental as Hartley ever got; or, if he ever felt more sentiment, he concealed it carefully.

"I s'pose it must 'a' been in spring that those old chaps, on their steeds and in their steel shirts, started out for the Holy Land or to rescue some damsel, hey?" he ended, with a grin. "Now, that's the way I feel—just like striking out for, say, Oshkosh. This has been a big strike here, sure's you live; that little piece of lofty tumbling was a big boom, and no mistake. Why, your share o' this campaign will be a hundred and twenty dollars sure."

"More'n I've earned," replied Bert.

"No, it ain't. You've done your duty like a man. Done as much in your way as I have. Now, if you want to try another county with me, say so. I'll make a thousand dollars this year out o' this thing."

"I guess I'll go back to school."

"All right; don't blame you at all."

"I guess, with what I can earn for father, I can pull through the year, I *must* get back. I'm awfully obliged to you, Jim."

"That'll do on that," said Hartley shortly; "you don't owe me anything. We'll finish delivery to-morrow, and be ready to pull out on Friday or Sat."

There was an acute pain in Albert's breast somewhere; he had not analyzed his case at all, and did not now, but the idea of going affected him strongly. It had been so pleasant, that daily return to a lovely girlish presence.

"Yes, sir," Hartley was going on; "I'm going to just quietly leave a book on her center table. I don't know as it'll interest her much, but it'll show we appreciate the grub, and so on. By jinks! You don't seem to realize what a worker that woman is. Up five o'clock in the morning—By the way, you've been going around with the girl a good deal, and she's introduced you to some first-rate sales; now, if you want 'o leave her a little something, make it a morocco copy, and charge it to the firm."

Albert knew that he meant well, but he couldn't, somehow, help saying ironically:

"Thanks; but I guess *one* copy of Blaine's 'Twenty Years' will be enough in the house, especially—"

"Well, give her anything you please, and charge it up to the firm. I don't insist on Blaine; only suggested that because—"

"I guess I can stand the expense of my own."

"I didn't say you couldn't, man! But *I* want a hand in this thing. Don't be so turrible keen t' snap a feller up," said Hartley, turning on him. "What the thunder is the matter of you anyway? I like the girl, and she's been good to us all round; she tended you like an angel—"

"There, there! That's enough o' that," put in Albert hastily. "F'r God's sake don't whang away on that string forever, as if I didn't know it!"

Hartley stared at him as he turned away.

"Well, by jinks! What *is* the matter o' you?"

He was too busy to dwell upon it much, but concluded his partner was homesick.

Albert was beginning to have a vague under-consciousness of his real feeling toward the girl, but he fought off the acknowledgment of it as long as possible. His mind moved in a circle, coming back to the one point ceaselessly—a dreary prospect, in which the slender girl-figure had no place—and each time the prospect grew more intolerably blank, and the pain in his heart more acute and throbbing.

When he faced her that night, after they had returned from a final skating party down on the river, he was as far from a solution as ever. He had avoided all reference to their separation, and now he stood as a man might at the parting of two paths, saying: "I will not choose; I can not choose. I will wait for some sign, some chance thing, to direct me."

They stood opposite each other, each feeling that there was more to be said; the girl tender, her eyes cast down, holding her hands to the fire; he shivering, but not with cold. He had a vague knowledge of the vast importance of the moment, and he hesitated to speak.

"It's almost spring again, isn't it? And you've been here—" she paused and looked up with a daring smile—"seems as if you'd been here always."

It was about half past eight. Mrs. Welsh was setting her bread in the kitchen; they could hear her moving about. Hartley was downtown finishing up his business.

Albert's throat grew dry and his limbs trembled. His pause was ominous; the girl's smile died away as he took a seat without looking at her.

"Well, Maud, I suppose—you know—we're going away to-morrow."

"Oh, must you? But you'll come back?"

"I don't expect to—I don't see how."

"Oh, don't say that!" cried the girl, her face as white as silver, her clasped hands straining.

"I must—I must!" he muttered, not looking at her, not daring to see her face.

"Oh, what can I do—*we* do, without you! I can't bear it!"

She stopped and sank back into a chair, her breath coming heavily from her twitching lips, the unnoticed tears falling from her staring, pitiful, wild, appealing eyes, her hands nervously twisting her gloves.

There was a long silence. Each was undergoing a self-revelation; each was trying to face a future without the other.

"I must go!" he repeated aimlessly, mechanically.

The girl's heavy breathing deepened into a wild little moaning sound, inexpressibly pitiful, her hungry eyes fixed on his face. She gave way first, and flung herself down upon her knees at his side, her hands seeking his neck.

"Albert, I can't *live* without you now! Take me with you! Don't leave me!"

He stooped suddenly and took her in his arms, raised her, and kissed her hair.

"I didn't mean it, Maud; I'll never leave you—never! Don't cry!"

She drew his face down to hers and kissed it, then turned her face to his breast and laughed and cried. There was a silence; then joy and confidence came back again.

"I know now what you meant," the girl cried gayly, raising herself and looking into his face; "you were trying to scare me, and make me show how much I—cared for you—first!" There was a soft smile on her lips and a tender light in her eyes. "But I don't mind it."

"I guess I didn't know myself what I meant," he said, with a grave smile.

When Mrs. Welsh came in, they were sitting on the sofa, talking in low voices of their future. He was grave and subdued, while she was radiant with love and hope. The future had no terrors for her. All plans were good and successful now. But the boy unconsciously felt the gravity of life somehow deepened by his love.

"Why, Maud!" Mrs. Welsh exclaimed, "what is—"

"O mother, I'm so happy—just as happy as a bird!" she cried, rushing into her mother's arms.

"Why, why!—what is it? You're crying, dear!"

"No, I'm not; I'm laughing—see!"

Mrs. Welsh turned her dim eyes on the girl, who shook the tears from her lashes with the action of a bird shaking water from its wings. She seemed to shake off her trouble at the same moment. Mrs. Welsh understood perfectly.

"I'm very glad, too, dearie," she said simply, looking at the young man with motherly love irradiating her worn face. Albert went to her, and she kissed him, while the happy girl put her arms about them both in an ecstatic hug.

"*Now* you've got a son, mother."

"But I've lost a daughter—my first-born."

"Oh, wait till you hear our plans!"

"He's going to settle down here—aren't you, Albert?"

Then they sat down, all three, and had a sweet, intimate talk of an hour, full of plans and hopes and confidences.

At last he kissed the radiant girl good night and, going into his own room, sat down by the stove and, watching the flicker of the flames through the chinks, pondered on the change that had come into his life.

Already he sighed with the stress of care, the press of thought, which came upon him. The longing uneasiness of the boy had given place to another unrest—the unrest of the man who must face the world in earnest now, planning for food and shelter; and all plans included Maud.

To go back to school was out of the question. To expect help from his father, overworked and burdened with debt, was impossible. He must go to work, and go to work to aid *her*. A living must be wrung from this town. All the home and all the property Mrs. Welsh had were here, and wherever Maud went the mother must follow; she could not live without her.

He was in the midst of the turmoil when Hartley came in, humming the "Mulligan Guards."

"In the dark, hey?"

"Completely in the dark."

"Well, light up, light up!"

"I'm trying to."

"What the deuce do you mean by that tone? What's been going on here since my absence?"

Albert did not reply, and Hartley shuffled about after a match, lighted the lamp, threw his coat and hat in the corner, and then said:

"Well, I've got everything straightened up. Been freezing out old Daggett; the old skeesix has been promisin' f'r a week, and I just said, 'Old man, I'll camp right down with you here till you fork over,' and he did. By the way, everybody I talked with to-day about leaving said, 'What's Lohr going to do with that girl?' I told 'em I didn't know; do you? It seems you've been thicker'n I supposed."

"I'm going to marry her," said Albert calmly, but his voice sounded strangely alien.

"What's that?" yelled Hartley.

"Sh! don't raise the neighbors. I'm going to marry her." He spoke quietly, but there was a peculiar numbness creeping over him.

"Well, by jinks! When? Say, looky here! Well, I swanny!" exclaimed Hartley helplessly. "When?"

"Right away; some time this summer—June, maybe."

Hartley thrust his hands into his trousers pockets, stretched out his legs, and stared at his friend in vast amaze.

"You're givin' me guff!"

"I'm in dead earnest."

"I thought you was going through college all so fast?"

"Well, I've made up my mind it ain't much use to try," replied Albert listlessly.

"What y' goin' t' do here, or are y' goin' t' take the girl away with yeh?"

"She can't leave her mother. We'll run this boarding house for the present. I'll try for the principalship of the school here. Raff is going to resign, he says; if I can't get that, I'll get into a law office here. Don't worry about me."

"But why go into this so quick? Why not put it off fifteen or twenty years?" asked Hartley, trying to get back to cheerful voice.

"What would be the use? At the end of a year I'd be just about as poor as I am now."

"Can't y'r father step in and help you?"

"No. There are three boys and two girls, all younger than I, to be looked out for, and he has all he can carry. Besides, *she* needs me right here and right now. Two delicate women struggling along; suppose one of 'em should fall sick? I tell you they need me, and if I can do anything to make life easy, or easier, I'm going t' do it. Besides," he ended in a peculiar tone, "we don't feel as if we could live apart much longer."

"But, great Scott! man, you can't—"

"Now, hold on, Jim! I've thought this thing all over, and I've made up my mind. It ain't any use to go on talking about it.

What good would it do me to go to school another year, come out without a dollar, and no more fitted for earning a living for her than I am now? And, besides all that, I couldn't draw a free breath thinking of her here workin' away to keep things moving, liable at any minute to break down."

Hartley gazed at him in despair, and with something like awe. It was a tremendous transformation in the young, ambitious student. He felt in a way responsible for the calamity, and that he ought to use every effort to bring the boy to his senses.

Like most men in America, and especially Western men, he still clung to the idea that a man was entirely responsible for his success or failure in life. He had not admitted that conditions of society might be so adverse that only men of most exceptional endowments, and willing and able to master many of the best and deepest and most sacred of their inspirations and impulses, could succeed.

Of the score of specially promising young fellows who had been with him at school, seventeen had dropped out and down. Most of them had married and gone back to farming, or to earn a precarious living in the small, dull towns where farmers trade and traders farm. Conditions were too adverse; they simply weakened and slipped slowly back into dullness and an oxlike or else a fretful patience. Thinking of these men, and thinking their failure due to themselves alone, Hartley could not endure the idea of his friend adding one more to the list of failures. He sprang up at last.

"Say, Bert, you might just as well hang y'rself, and done with it! Why, it's suicide! I can't allow it. I started in at college bravely, and failed because I'd let it go too long. I couldn't study—couldn't get down to it; but you—why, old man, I'd *bet* on you!" He had a tremor in his voice. "I hate like thunder to see you give up your plans. Say, you can't afford to do this; it's too much to pay."

"No, it ain't."

"I say it is. What do you get, in—"

"I think so much o' her that—"

"Oh, nonsense! You'd get over this in a week."

"Jim!" called Albert warningly, sharply.

"All right," said Jim, in the tone of a man who felt that it was all wrong—"all right; but the time'll come when you'll wish I'd—You ain't doin' the girl enough good to make up for the harm you're doin' yourself." He broke off again, and said in a tone of peculiar meaning: "I'm done. I'm all through, and I c'n see you're through with Jim Hartley. Why, Bert, look here—No? All right!"

"Darn curious," he muttered to himself, "that boy should get caught just at this time, and not with some one o' those girls in Marion. Well, it's none o' my funeral," he ended, with a sigh; for it had stirred him to the bottom of his sunny nature, after all. A dozen times, as he lay there beside his equally sleepless companion, he started to say something more in deprecation of the step, but each time stifled the opening word into a groan.

It would not be true to say that love had come to Albert Lohr as a relaxing influence, but it had changed the direction of his energies so radically as to make his whole life seem weaker and lower. As long as his love-dreams went out toward a vague and ideal woman, supposedly higher and grander than himself, he was spurred on to face the terrible sheer escarpment of social eminence; but when he met, by accident, the actual woman who was to inspire his future efforts, the difficulties he faced took on solid reality.

His aspirations fell to the earth, their wings clipped, and became, perforce, submissive beasts at the plow. The force that moved so much of his thought was transformed into other energy. Whether it were a wise step or not he did not know; he certainly knew it was right.

The table was very gay at dinner next day. Maud was standing at the highest point of her girlhood dreams. Her flushed face and shining eyes made her seem almost a child, and Hartley wondered at her, and relented a little in the face of such happiness. Her face was turned to Albert in an unconscious, beautiful way; she had nothing to conceal now.

Mrs. Welsh was happy, too, but a little tearful in an unobtrusive way. Troutt had his jokes, of course, not very delicate, but of good intention. In fact, they were as flags and trumpets to the young people. Mrs. Welsh had confided in him, telling him to be secret; but the finesse of his joking could not fail to reveal everything he knew.

But Maud cared little. She was filled with a sort of tender boldness; and Albert, in the delight of the hour, gave himself up wholly to a trust in the future and to the fragrance and music of love.

"They're gay as larks now," thought Hartley to himself, as he joined in the laughter; "but that won't help 'em any, ten years from now."

He could hardly speak next day as he shook hands at the station with his friend.

"Good-by, ol' man; I hope it'll come out all right, but I'm afraid—But there! I promised not to say anything about it. Good-by till we meet in Congress," he ended in a lamentable attempt at being funny.

"Can't you come to the wedding, Jim? We've decided on June. You see, they need a man around the house, so we—You'll come, won't you, old fellow? And don't mind my being a little crusty last night."

"Oh, yes; I'll come," Jim said, in a tone which concealed a desire to utter one more protest.

"It's no use; that ends him, sure's I'm a thief. He's jumped into a hole and pulled the hole in after him. A man can't marry a family like that at his age, and pull out of it. He *may*, but I doubt it. Well, as I remarked before, it's none o' my funeral so long as *he's* satisfied."

But he said it with a painful lump in his throat, and he could not bring himself to feel that Albert's course was right, and felt himself to be somehow culpable in the case.

AN ALIEN IN THE PINES

I

A man and a woman were pacing up and down the wintry station platform, waiting for a train. On every side the snow lay a stained and crumpled blanket, with here and there a light or a chimney to show the village sleeping beneath.

The sky was a purple-black hemisphere, out of which the stars glittered almost white. The wind came out of the west, cold but amiable; the cracked bell of a switch engine gurgled querulously at intervals, followed by the bumping of coupling freight cars; roosters were crowing, and sleepy train men were assembling in sullen silence.

The couple walked with arms locked like lovers, but the tones of their voices had the quality which comes after marriage. They were man and wife.

The woman's clear voice arose. "O Ed, isn't this delicious? What one misses by not getting up early!"

"Sleep, for instance," laughed her husband.

"Don't drag me down. You know what I mean. Let's get up

early every morning while we're up here in the woods."

"Shouldn't wonder if we had to. There'll be a lot to do, and I want to get back to Chicago by the 1st of February."

"This is an experience! Isn't it still? When is our train due?"

"Due now; I think that is our headlight up the track."

As he spoke, an engine added its voice to the growing noise of the station, and drew solemnly down the frosty steel.

An eruption of shapeless forms of men from the depot filled the one general coach of the train. They nearly all were dressed in some sort of fur coat, and all had the look of men accustomed to outdoor life—powerful, loud-voiced, unrefined. They were, in fact, traveling men, business men, the owners of mills or timber. The stolid or patient oxlike faces of some Norwegian workmen, dressed in gay Mackinac jackets, were sprinkled about.

The young wife was a fine type of woman anywhere, but these surroundings made her seem very dainty and startlingly beautiful. Her husband had the fair skin of a city man, but his powerful shoulders and firm step denoted health and wholesome living. They were good to see as man and wife.

They soon felt the reaction to sleepiness which comes to those not accustomed to early rising, and the wife, soothed by the clank of the train, leaned her head on her husband's shoulder and dozed. He looked out upon the landscape, glad that his wife was not observing it. He did not know such desolation existed in Wisconsin.

On every side were the evidences of a ruined forest land. A landscape of flat wastes, of thinned and burned and uprooted trees. A desolate and apparently useless land.

Here and there a sawmill stood gray and sagging, surrounded by little cabins of unpainted wood, to testify to the time when great pines stood all about, and the ring of the swamper's axe was heard in the intervals of silence between the howls of a saw.

To the north the swells grew larger. Birch and tamarack swamps alternated with dry ridges on which an inferior pine still grew. The swamps were dense tangles of broken and uprooted trees. Slender pikelike stumps of fire-devastated firs rose here and there, black and grim skeletons of trees.

It was a land that had been sheared by the axe, torn by the winds, and blasted by fire.

Off to the west low blue ridges rose, marking the boundaries of the valley which had been washed out ages ago by water. After the floods it had sprung up to pine forests, and these in their turn had been sheared away by man. It lay now awaiting the plow and seeder of the intrepid pioneer.

Suddenly the wife roused up. "Why, we haven't had any breakfast!"

He smiled at her childish look of bewilderment. "I've been painfully aware of it for some time back. I've been suffering for food while you slept."

"Why didn't you get into the basket?"

"How could I, with you on my manly bosom?"

She colored up a little. They had not been married long, evidently.

Hamlin Garland

They were soon eating a breakfast with the spirit of picknickers. Occasionally she looked out of the window.

"What a wild country!" she said. He did not emphasize its qualities to her; rather, he distracted her attention from the desolation.

The train roared round its curves, conforming with the general course of the river. On every hand were thickening signs of active lumber industry. They flashed by freight trains loaded with logs or lumber or ties. Mills in operation grew thicker.

The car echoed with the talk of lumber. A brisk man with a red mustache was exhibiting a model of a machine to cut certain parts of machinery out of "two by fours." Another was describing a new shingle mill he had just built.

A couple of elderly men, one a German, were discussing the tariff on lumber. The workmen mainly sat silent.

"It's all so strange!" the young wife said again and again.

"Yes, it isn't exactly the Lake Shore drive."

"I like it. I wish I could smell the pines."

"You'll have all the pines you can stand before we get back to Chicago."

"No, sir; I'm going to enjoy every moment of it; and you're going to let me help, you know—look over papers and all that. I'm the heiress, you must remember," she said wickedly.

"Well, we won't quarrel about that until we see how it all turns out. It may not be worth my time up here. I shall charge you roundly as your lawyer; depend on that."

The outlook grew more attractive as the train sped on. Old Mosinee rose, a fine rounded blue shape, on the left.

"Why, there's a mountain! I didn't know Wisconsin had such a mountain as that."

"Neither did I. This valley is fine. Now, if your uncle's estates only included that hill!"

The valley made off to the northwest with a bold, large, and dignified movement. The coloring, blue and silver, purple-brown and bronze-green, was suitable to the grouping of lines. It was all fresh and vital, wholesome and very impressive.

From this point the land grew wilder—that is, more primeval: There was more of Nature and less of man. The scar of the axe was here and there, but the forest predominated. The ridges of pine foliages broke against the sky miles and miles in splendid sweep.

"This must be lovely in summer," the wife said, again and again, as they flashed by some lake set among the hills.

"It's fine now," he replied, feeling the thrill of the sportsman. "I'd like to shoulder a rifle and plunge into those snowy vistas. How it brings the wild spirit out in a man! Women never feel that delight."

"Oh, yes, we do," she replied, glad that something remained yet unexplained between them. "We feel just like men, only we haven't the strength of mind to demand a share of it with you."

"Yes, you feel it at this distance. You'd come back mighty quick the second night out."

She did not relish his laughter, and so looked away out of the window. "Just think of it—Uncle Edwin lived here thirty years!"

He forbore to notice her inconsistency. "Yes, the wilderness is all right for a vacation, but I prefer Chicago for the year round."

When they came upon Ridgeley, both cried out with delight.

"Oh, what a dear, picturesque little town!" she said.

"Well, well! I wonder how they came to build a town without a row of battlemented stores?"

It lay among and upon the sharp, low, stumpy pine ridges in haphazard fashion, like a Swiss village. A small brook ran through it, smothered here and there in snow. A sawmill was the largest figure of the town, and the railway station was the center. There was not an inch of painted board in the village. Everywhere the clear yellow of the pine flamed unstained by time. Lumber piles filled all the lower levels near the creek. Evidently the town had been built along logging roads, and there was something grateful and admirable in its irregular arrangement. The houses, moreover, were all modifications of the logging camps; even the drug store stood with its side to the street. All about were stumps and fringes of pines, which the lumbermen, for some good reason, had passed by. Charred boles stood purple-black out of the snow.

It was all green and gray and blue and yellow-white and wild. The sky was not more illimitable than the rugged forest which extended on every hand.

"Oh, this is glorious—glorious!" said the wife. "Do I own some of this town?" she asked, as they rose to go out.

"I reckon you do."

"Oh, I'm so glad!"

As they stepped out on the platform, a large man in corduroy and wolf-skin faced them like a bandit.

"Hello, Ed!"

"Hello, Jack! Well, we've found you. My wife, Mr. Ridgeley. We've come up to find out how much you've embezzled," he said, as Ridgeley pulled off an immense glove to shake hands all round.

"Well, come right over to the hotel. It ain't the Auditorium, but then, again, it ain't like sleeping outdoors."

As they moved along they heard the train go off, and then the sound of the saw resumed its domination of the village noises.

"Was the town named after you, or you after the town?" asked Field.

"Named after me. Old man didn't want it named after him; would kill it," he said.

Mr. and Mrs. Field found the hotel quite comfortable and the dinner wholesome. They beamed upon each other.

"It's going to be delightful," they said.

Ridgeley was a bachelor, and found his home at the hotel

also. That night he said: "Now we'll go over the papers and records of your uncle's property, and then we'll go out and see if the property is all there. I imagine this is to be a searching investigation."

"You may well think it. My wife is inexorable."

As night fell, the wife did not feel so safe and well pleased. The loud talking in the office below and the occasional whooping of a crowd of mill hands going by made her draw her chair nearer and lay her fingers in her husband's palm.

He smiled indulgently. "Don't be frightened, my dear. These men are not half so bad as they sound."

II

Mrs. Field sat in the inner room of Ridgeley's office, waiting for the return of her husband with the team. They were going out for a drive.

Ridgeley was working at his books, and he had forgotten her presence.

She could not but feel a deep admiration for his powerful frame and his quick, absorbed action as he moved about from his safe to his desk. He was a man of great force and ready decision.

Suddenly the door opened and a man entered. He had a sullen and bitter look on his thin, dark face. Ridgeley's quick eyes measured him, and his hand softly turned the key in his money drawer, and as he faced about he swung shut the door of the safe.

The stranger saw all this with eyes as keen as Ridgeley's. A cheerless and strange smile came upon his face.

"Don't be alarmed," he said. "I'm low, but I ain't as low as that."

"Well, sir, what can I do for you?" asked Ridgeley. Mrs. Field half rose, and her heart beat terribly. She felt something tense and strange in the attitude of the two men.

But the man only said, "You can give me a job if you want to."

Ridgeley remained alert. He ran his eyes over the man's tall frame. He looked strong and intelligent, although his eyes

Hamlin Garland

were fevered and dull.

"What kind of a job?"

"Any kind that will take me out into the woods and keep me there," the man replied.

There was a self-accusing tone in his voice that Ridgeley felt.

"What's your object? You look like a man who could do something else. What brings you here?"

The man turned with a sudden resolution to punish himself. His voice expressed a terrible loathing.

"Whisky, that's what. It's a hell of a thing to say, but I can't let liquor alone when I can smell it. I'm no common hand, or I wouldn't be if I—But let that go. I can swing an axe, and I'm ready to work. That's enough. Now the question is, can you find a place for me?"

Ridgeley mused a little. The young fellow stood there, statuesque, rebellious.

Then Ridgeley said, "I guess I can help you out that much." He picked up a card and a pencil. "What shall I call you?"

"Oh, call me Williams; that ain't my name, but it'll do."

"What you been doing?"

"Everything part of the time, drinking the rest. Was in a livery stable down at Wausau last week. It came over me, when I woke yesterday, that I was gone to hell if I stayed in town. So I struck out; and I don't care for myself, but I've got a woman to look out for—" He stopped abruptly. His recklessness of mood had its limits, after all.

Ridgeley penciled on a card. "Give this to the foreman of No. 6. The men over at the mill will show you the teams."

The man started toward the door with the card in his hand. He turned suddenly.

"One thing more. I want you to send ten dollars of my pay every two weeks to this address." He took an envelope out of his pocket. "It don't matter what I say or do after this, I want that money sent. The rest will keep me in tobacco and clothing. You understand?"

Ridgeley nodded. "Perfectly. I've seen such cases before."

The man went out and down the walk with a hurried, determined air, as if afraid of his own resolution.

As Ridgeley turned toward his desk he met Mrs. Field, who faced him with tears of fervent sympathy in her eyes.

"Isn't it awful?" she said, in a half whisper. "Poor fellow, what will become of him?"

"Oh, I don't know. He'll get along some way. Such fellows do. I've had 'em before. They try it a while here; then they move. I can't worry about them."

Mrs. Field was not listening to his shifty words. "And then, think of his wife—how she must worry."

Ridgeley smiled. "Perhaps it's his mother or a sister."

"Anyway it's awful. Can't something be done for him?"

"I guess we've done about all that can be done."

"Oh, I wish I could help him! I'll tell Ed about him."

"Don't worry about him, Mrs. Field; he ain't worth it."

"Oh yes, he is. I feel he's been a good boy once, and then he's so self-accusing."

Her own happiness was so complete, she could not bear to think of others' misery. She told her husband about Williams, and ended by asking, "Can't we do anything to help the poor fellow?"

Field was not deeply concerned. "No; he's probably past help. Such men are so set in their habits, nothing but a miracle or hypnotism can save them. He'll end up as a 'lumber Jack,' as the townsmen call the hands in the camps."

"But he isn't that, Edward. He's finer some way. You feel he is. Ask Mr. Ridgeley."

Ridgeley merely said: "Yes, he seemed to me to be more than a common hand. But, all the same, it won't be two weeks before he'll be in here as drunk as a wild cat, wanting to shoot me for holding back his money."

In this way Williams came to be to Mrs. Field a very important figure in the landscape of that region. She often spoke of him, and on the following Saturday night, when Field came home, she anxiously asked, "Is Williams in town?"

"No, he hasn't shown up yet."

She clapped her hands in delight. "Good! good! He's going

to win his fight."

Field laughed. "Don't bet on Williams too soon. We'll hear from him before the week is out."

"When are we going to visit the camp?" she asked, changing the subject.

"As soon as it warms up a little. It is too cold for you."

She had a laugh at him. "You were the one who wanted to 'plunge into the snowy vistas.'"

He evaded her joke on him by assuming a careless tone. "I'm not plunging as much as I was; the snow is too deep."

"When you go I want to go with you—I want to see Williams."

"Ha!" he snorted melodramatically. "She scorns me faithful heart. She turns—"

Mrs. Field smiled faintly. "Don't joke about it Ed. I can't get that wife out of my mind."

III

A few very cold gray days followed, and then the north wind cleared the sky; and, though it was still cold, it was pleasant. The sky had only a small white cloud here and there to make its blueness the more profound.

Ridgeley dashed up to the door with a hardy little pair of bronchos hitched to a light pair of bobs, and Mrs. Field was tucked in like a babe in a cradle.

Almost the first thing she asked was, "How is Williams?"

"Oh, he's getting on nicely. He refused to sleep with his bunk mate, and finally had to lick him, I understand, to shut him up. Challenged the whole camp then to let him alone or take a licking. They let him alone, Lawson says.—G'lang there, you rats!"

Mrs. Field said no more, for the air was whizzing by her ears, and she hardly dared look out, so keen was the wind, but as soon as they entered the deeps of the forest it was profoundly still.

The ride that afternoon was a glory she never forgot. Everywhere yellow-greens and purple shadows. The sun in a burnished blue sky flooded the forests with light, striking down through even the thickest pines to lay in fleckings of radiant white and gold upon the snow.

The trail (it was not a road) ran like a graceful furrow over the hills, around little lakes covered deep with snow, through tamarack swamps where the tracks of wild things thickened, over ridges of tall pine clear of brush, and curving every-where amid stumps, where dismantled old shanties marked the site of the older logging camps. Sometimes they met teams going to the store. Sometimes they crossed logging roads—wide, smooth tracks artificially iced, down which mountainous loads of logs were slipping, creaking and groaning. Sometimes they heard the dry click-clock of the woodsmen's axes, or the crash of falling trees deep in the wood. When they reached the first camp, Ridgeley pulled up the steaming horses at the door and shouted, "Hello, the camp!"

A tall old man with a long red beard came out. He held one bare red arm above his eyes. He wore an apron.

"Hello, Sandy!"

"Hello, Mr. Ridgeley!"

"Ready for company?"

"Am always ready for company," he said, with a Scotch accent.

"Well, we're coming in to get warm."

"Vera wal."

As they went in, under the roofed shed between the cook's shanty and the other and larger shanty, Mrs. Field sniffed. Sandy led them past a large pyramid composed of the scraps of beef bones, eggshells, cans, and tea grounds left over during the winter. In the shed itself hung great slabs of beef.

It was as untidy and suggestive of slaughter as the nest of a brood of eagles.

Sandy was beginning dinner on a huge stove spotted with rust and pancake batter. All about was the litter of his preparation. Beef—beef on all sides, and tin dishes and bare benches and huge iron cooking pans.

Mrs. Field was glad to get out into the sunlight again.

"What a horrible place! Are they all like that?"

"No, my camps are not like that—or, I should say, *our* camps," Ridgeley added, with a smile.

"Not a gay place at all," said Field, in exaggerated reserve.

But Mrs. Field found her own camps not much better. True, the refuse was not raised in pyramidal shape before the front door, and the beef was a little more orderly, but the low log huts, the dim cold light, the dingy walls and floors, the lack of any womanly or home touch, the tin dishes, the wholesale cooking, all struck upon her with terrible force.

"Do human beings live here?" she asked Ridgeley, when he opened the door of the main shanty of No. 6.

"Forty creatures of the men kind sleep and house here," he replied.

"To which the socks and things give evidence," said Field promptly, pointing toward the huge stove which sat like a rusty-red cheese in the center of the room. Above it hung scores of ragged gray and red socks and Mackinac boots and jackets which had been washed by the men themselves.

Around were the grimy bunks where the forty men slept like tramps in a steamer's hold. The quilts were grimy, and the posts greasy and shining with the touch of hands. There were no chairs—only a kind of rude stool made of boards. There were benches near the stove nailed to the rough floor. In each bunk, hanging to a peg, was the poor little imitation-leather hand-bag which contained the whole wardrobe of each man, exclusive of the tattered socks and shirts hanging over the stove.

The room was chill and cold and gray. It had only two small windows. Its doors were low. Even Mrs. Field was forced to stoop in entering. This made it seem more like a den. There were roller towels in the corner, and washbasins, and a grindstone, which made it seem like a barn. It was, in fact, more cheerless than the barn, and less wholesome.

"Doesn't that hay in the bunks get a—a—sometimes?" asked Field.

"Well, yes, I shouldn't wonder, though the men are pretty strict about that. They keep pretty free from that, I think. However, I shouldn't want to run no river chances on the thing myself." Ridgeley smiled at Mrs. Field's shudder of horror.

"Is this the place?" The men laughed. She had asked that question so many times before.

"Yes, *this* is where Mr. Williams hangs out.—Say, Field, you'll need to make some new move to hold your end up against Williams."

Mrs. Field felt hurt and angry at his rough joke. In the dim corner a cough was heard, and a yellow head raised itself over the bunk board ghastily. His big blue eyes fixed themselves on the lovely woman and he wore a look of childish wonder.

"Hello, Gus—didn't see you. What's the matter—sick?"

"Yah, ai baen hwick two days. Ai tank ai lack to hav doketer."

"All right, I'll send him up. What seems the matter?"

As they talked, Mrs. Field again chilled with the cold gray comfortlessness of it all; to be sick in such a place! The strange appearance of the man out of his grim corner was startling. She was glad when they drove out into the woods again, where the clear sunshine fell, and the pines stood against the blazing winter sky motionless as iron trees. Her pleasure in the ride was growing less. To her delicate sense this life was sordid, not picturesque. She wondered how Williams endured it. They arrived at No. 8 just as the men were trailing down the road to work after eating their dinner. Their gay-colored jackets of Mackinac wool stood out like trumpet notes in the prevailing white and blue and bronze green.

The boss and the scaler came out and met them, and after introductions they went into the shanty to dinner. The cook was a deft young Norwegian—a clean, quick, gentlemanly young fellow with a fine brown mustache. He cleared a place for them at one end of the long table, and they sat down.

It was a large camp, but much like the others. On the table were the same cheap iron forks, the tin plates, and the small tin basins (for tea) which made up the dinner set. Basins of brown sugar stood about.

"Good gracious! Do people still eat brown sugar? Why, I haven't seen any of that for ages," cried Mrs. Field.

The stew was good and savory, and the bread fair. The tea was not all clover, but it tasted of the tin. Mrs. Field said:

"Beef, beef, everywhere beef. One might suppose a menagerie of desert animals ate here. Edward, we must make things more comfortable for our men. They must have cups to drink out of; these basins are horrible."

It was humorous to the men, this housewifely suggestion.

"Oh, make it napkins, Allie!"

"You can laugh, but I sh'an't rest after seeing this. If you thought I was going to say, 'Oh, how picturesque!' you're mistaken. I think it's barbarous."

She was getting impatient of their patronizing laughter, as if she were a child. They changed their manner to one of acquiescence, but thought of her as a child just the same.

After dinner they all went out to see the crew working. It was the biggest crew anywhere in the neighborhood, and they sat a long while and watched the men at work. Ridgeley got out and hitched the team to a tree, and took Field up to the skidway. Mrs. Field remained in the sleigh, however.

Near her "the swamping team," a span of big deep-red oxen, came and went among the green tops of the fallen pines. They crawled along their trails in the snow like some strange machinery, and the boy in a blue jacket moved almost as listlessly. Somewhere in the tangle of refuse boughs the swampers' axes click-clocked, saws uttered their grating, rhythmic snarl, and great trees at intervals shivered, groaned, and fell with soft, rushing, cracking sweeps into the deep snow, and the swampers swarmed upon them like Lilliputians attacking a giant enemy.

There was something splendid (though tragic) in the work, but the thought of the homelessness of the men, their terrible beds, and their long hours of toil oppressed the delicate and refined woman. She began to take on culpability. She was partly in authority now, and this system must be changed. She was deep in plans for change, in shanties and in sleeping places, when the men returned.

Ridgeley was saying: "No, we control about thirty thousand acres of pine as good as that. It ain't what it was twenty years ago, but it's worth money, after all."

It was getting near to dark as they reached No. 6 again, and Ridgeley drew up and helped them out and into the cook's shanty.

Mrs. Field was introduced to the cook, a short, rather sullen, but intelligent man. He stood over the red-hot stove, laying great slices of beef in a huge dripping-pan. He had a taffler or assistant in the person of a half-grown boy, at whom he jerked rough orders like hunks of stove wood. Some hit the boy and produced noticeable effects, others did not.

Meanwhile a triumphant sunset was making the west one splendor of purple and orange and crimson, which came over the cool green rim of the pines like the Valhalla March in Wagner.

Mrs. Field sat there in the dim room by the window, seeing that splendor flush and fade, and thinking how dangerous it was to ask where one's wealth comes from in the world. Outside, the voices of the men thickened; they were dropping in by twos and fours, with teams and on foot.

The assistant arranged the basins in rows, and put one of the iron forks and knives on each side of each plate, and filled the sugar-basins and dumped in the cold beans, and split the bread into slabs, and put small pots of tea here and there ready for the hands of the men.

At last, when the big pans of toast, the big plates of beef, were placed steaming on the table, the cook called Field and Ridgeley and said:

"Set right here at the end." He raised his arm to a ring which dangled on a wire. "Now look out; you'll see 'em come sidewise." He jerked the ring and disappeared into the kitchen.

There came shouts, trampling, laughter, and the door burst open and they streamed in—Norwegians, French, half-breeds, dark-skinned fellows all of them save the Norwegians. They came like a flood, but they fell silent at sight of a woman, so beautiful and strange to them.

All words ceased. They sank into place beside the table with the thump of falling sandbags. They were all in their shirt sleeves, but they were cleanly washed, and the most of them had combed their hair; but they seemed very wild and hairy to Mrs. Field. She looked at her husband and Ridgeley with a grateful pleasure; it was so restful to have them on each side of her.

The men ate like hungry dogs. They gorged in silence. Nothing was heard but the clank of knives on tin plates, the drop of heavy plates of food, and the occasional muttered words of some one asking for the bread and the gravy.

As they ate they furtively looked with great curiosity and admiration up at the dainty woman. Their eyes were bright and large, and gleamed out of the obscure brown of their dimly lighted faces with savage intensity—so it seemed to Mrs. Field, and she dropped her eyes upon her plate.

Her husband and Ridgeley entered into conversation with

Hamlin Garland

those sitting near. Ridgeley seemed on good terms with them all, and ventured a joke or word, at which they laughed with terrific energy, and fell as suddenly silent again.

As Mrs. Field looked up the second time she saw the dark, strange face of Williams a few places down, and opposite her. His eyes were fixed on her husband's hands with a singular intensity. Her eyes followed his, and the beauty of her husband's hands came to her again with new force. They were perfectly shaped, supple, warm-colored, and strong. Their color and deftness stood out in vivid contrast to the heavy, brown, cracked, and calloused pawlike hands of the men.

Why should Williams study her husband's hands? If he had looked at her she would not have been surprised. The other men she could read. They expressed either frank, simple admiration or furtive desire. But this man looked at her husband, and his eyes fell often upon his own hands, which trembled with fatigue. He handled his knife clumsily, and yet she could see he, too, had a fine hand—a slender, powerful hand like that people call an artist hand—a craftsmanlike hand.

He saw her looking at him, and he flashed one enigmatical glance into her eyes, and rose to go out.

"How you getting on, Williams?" Ridgeley asked.

Williams resented his question. "Oh, I'm all right," he said sullenly.

The meal was all over in an incredibly short time. One by one, two by two, they rose heavily and lumbered out with one last wistful look at Mrs. Field. She will never know how seraphic she seemed sitting there amid those rough surroundings—the dim red light of the kerosene lamp falling across her clear pallor, out of which her dark eyes shone with liquid softness, made deeper and darker by her half-sorrowful tenderness for these homeless fellows.

An hour later, as they were standing at the door, just ready to take to their sleigh, they heard the scraping of a fiddle.

"Oh, some one is going to play!" Mrs. Field cried, with visions of the rollicking good times she had heard so much about and of which she had seen nothing so far. "Can't I look in?"

Ridgeley was dubious. "I'll go and see," he said, and entered the door. "Boys, Mrs. Field wants to look in a minute. Go on with your fiddling, Sam—only I wanted to see that you weren't sitting around in dishabill."

This seemed a good joke, and they all howled and haw-hawed gleefully.

"So go right ahead with your evening prayers. All but—you understand!"

"All right, captain," said Sam, the man with the fiddle.

When Mrs. Field looked in, two men were furiously grinding axes; several were sewing on ragged garments; all were smoking; some were dressing chapped or bruised fingers. The atmosphere was horrible. The socks and shirts were steaming above the huge stove; the smoke and stench for a moment were sickening, but Ridgeley pushed them just inside the door.

"It's better out of the draught."

Sam jigged away on the violin. The men kept time with the

Hamlin Garland

cranks of the grindstone, and all hands looked up with their best smile at Mrs. Field. Most of them shrank a little from her look like shy animals.

Ridgeley threw open the window. "In the old days," he explained to Mrs. Field, "we used a fireplace, and that kept the air better."

As her sense of smell became deadened the air seemed a little more tolerable to Mrs. Field.

"Oh, we must change all this," she said. "It is horrible."

"Play us a tune," said Sam, extending the violin to Field. He did not think Field could play. It was merely a shot in the dark on his part.

Field took it and looked at it and sounded it. On every side the men turned face in eager expectancy.

"He can play, that feller."

"I'll bet he can. He handles her as if he knew her."

"You bet your life.—Tune up, Cap."

Williams came from the obscurity somewhere, and looked over the shoulders of the men.

"Down in front," somebody called, and the men took seats on the benches, leaving Field standing with the violin in hand. He smiled around upon them in a frank, pleased way, quite ready to show his skill. He played "Annie Laurie," and a storm of applause broke out.

"*Hoo*-ray! Bully for you!"

"Sam, you're out of it."

"Sam, your name is Mud."

"Give us another, Cap."

"It ain't the same fiddle."

He played again some simple tune, and he played it with the touch which showed the skilled amateur. As he played, Mrs. Field noticed a grave restlessness on Williams's part. He moved about uneasily. He gnawed at his finger nails. His eyes glowed with a singular fire. His hands drummed and fingered. At last he approached and said roughly:

"Let me take that fiddle a minute."

"Oh, cheese it, Williams!" the men cried. "Let the other man play."

"What do *you* want to do with the fiddle—think it's a music box?" asked Sam, its owner.

"Go to hell!" said Williams. As Field gave the violin over to him his hands seemed to tremble with eagerness.

He raised his bow and struck into an imposing brilliant strain, and the men fell back in astonishment.

"Well, I'll be damned!" gasped the owner of the violin.

"Keep quiet, Sam."

Mrs. Field looked at her husband. "Why, Ed, he is playing Sarasate!"

"That's what he is," he returned slangily, too much astonished to do more than gaze. Williams played on.

There was a faint defect in the high notes, as if his fingers did not touch the strings properly, but his bow action showed cultivation and breadth of feeling. As he struck into one of those difficult octave-leaping movements his face became savage. On the E string a squeal broke forth; he flung the violin into Sam's lap with a ferocious curse, and then extending his hands, hard, crooked to fit the axe-helve, calloused and chapped, he said to Field:

"Look at my cursed hands. Lovely things to play with, ain't they?"

His voice trembled with passion. He turned and went outside. As he passed Mrs. Field his head was bowed and he was uttering a groaning cry like one suffering acute physical agony.

She went out quickly, and Field and Ridgeley followed. They were all moved—but the men made little of it, seeing how deeply touched she was.

"That's what drink does for a man," Ridgeley said, as they watched Williams disappear down the swampers' trail.

"That man has been a violinist," said Field. "What's he doing up here?"

"Came up to get away from himself," Ridgeley replied.

"I'm afraid he's failed," said Field, as he put his arm about his wife and led her to the sleigh.

The ride home was made mainly in silence. "Oh, the splendid

silence!" the woman kept saying in her heart. "Oh, the splendid moonlight, the marvelous radiance!" Everywhere a heavenly serenity—not a footstep, not a bell, not a cry, not a cracking tree—nothing but vivid light, white snow dappled and lined with shadows, and trees etched against a starlit sky. Splendor of light and sheen and shadow. Wide wastes of snow so white the stumps stood like columns of charcoal. A night of Nature's making when she is tired of noise and blare of color.

And in the midst of it stood the camps and the reek of obscenity, foul odors, and tobacco smoke, to which a tortured soul must return.

IV

The following Saturday afternoon, as Ridgeley and Field entered the office, Williams rose to meet them. He looked different; finer some way, Field imagined. At any rate, he was perfectly sober. He was freshly shaven, and though his clothes were rough, he looked like a man of education. His manner was cold and distant.

"I'd like to be paid off, Mr. Ridgeley," he said. "I guess what's left of my pay will take me out of this."

"Where do you propose to go?" Ridgeley said kindly.

Williams must have perceived his kindliness, for he answered: "I'm going home to my wife. I am going to try it once more."

After Williams went out Field said, "I wonder if he'll do it?"

"Oh, I shouldn't wonder. I've seen men brace up just as mysteriously as that and stay right by their resolutions. I thought he didn't look like a common lumber Jack when he came in."

"Oh, how happy his wife will be!" Mrs. Field cried when she heard of Williams's resolution. "She'll save him yet."

"Well, I don't know; depends on what kind of a woman she is."

THE OWNER OF THE MILL FARM

Beyond his necessity, a tired man is not apt to be polite. This Mrs. Miner had generalized from long experience with her husband. She knew at a distance, by the way he wore his hat when he came in out of the field, whether he was in a peculiarly savage mood, or only in his usual state of sullen indifference.

As he came in out of the barn on this spring day, he turned to look up at the roof with a curse. Something had angered him. He did not stop to comb his hair after washing at the pump, but came into the neat kitchen and surlily took a seat at the table.

Mrs. Miner, a slender little woman, quite ladylike in appearance, had the dinner all placed in steaming abundance upon the table, and the children, sitting side by side, watched their father in silence. There was an air of foreboding, of apprehension, over them all, as if they feared some brutal outbreak on his part.

He placed his elbows on the table. His sleeves were rolled up, displaying his red and much sunburned arms. He wore no coat, and his face was sullen, and held, besides, a certain vicious quality, like that of a bad-tempered dog.

Hamlin Garland

He had not spoken to his wife directly for many weeks. For years it had been his almost constant habit to address her through the children, by calling her "she" or "your mother." He had done this so long that even the little ones were startled when he said, looking straight at her:

"Say, what are you going to do about that roof?"

Mrs. Miner turned her large gray eyes upon him in sudden confusion. "Excuse me, Tom, I didn't—"

"I said 'What you goin' t' do with that roof?'" he repeated brutally.

"What roof?" she asked timidly.

"What roof?" he repeated after her. "Why, the barn, of course! It's leakin' and rottin' my oats. It's none o' my business," he went on, his voice containing an undercurrent of vicious insult. "Only I thought you'd like to know it's worse than ever. You can do as you like about it," he said again, and there was a peculiar tone in his voice, as if, by using that tone, he touched her upon naked nerves somewhere. "I guess I can cover the oats up."

A stranger would not have known what it all meant, and yet there was something in what he said that made his wife turn white. But she answered quietly:

"I'll send word to the carpenter this forenoon. I'm sorry," she went on, the tears coming to her eyes. She turned away and looked out of the window, while he ate on indifferently. At last she turned with a sudden impulse: "O Tom, why can't we be friends again? For the children's sake, you ought to—"

"Oh, shut up!" he snarled. "Good God! Can't you let a thing

rest? Suits me well enough. I ain't complainin'. So, just shut up."

He rose with a slam and went out. The two children sat with hushed breath. They knew him too well to cry out.

Mrs. Miner sat for a long time at the table without moving. At last she rose and went sighfully at work. "Morty, I want you to run down to Mr. Wilber's and ask him to come up and see me about some work." She stood at the window and watched the boy as he stepped lightly down the road. "How much he looks like his father, in spite of his sunny temper!" she thought, and it was not altogether a pleasant thing to think of, though she did not allow such a thought to take definite shape.

The young carpenter whom Wilber sent to fill Mrs. Miner's order walked with the gay feet of youth as he passed out of the little town toward the river. When he came to the bridge, he paused and studied the scene with slow, delighted eyes. The water came down over its dam with a leap of buoyant joy, as if leaping to freedom. Over the dam it lay in a quiet pool, mirroring every bud and twig. Below, it curved away between low banks, with bushes growing to the water's edge, where the pickerel lay.

But the young man seemed to be saddened by the view of the mill, which had burned some years before. It seemed like the charred body of a living thing, this heap of blackened and twisted shafts and pulleys, lying half buried in tangles of weeds.

It appealed so strongly to young Morris that he uttered an unconscious sigh as he walked on across the bridge and clambered the shelving road, which was cut out of the yellow sandstone of the hillside.

The road wound up the sandy hillside and came at length to a beautiful broad terrace of farm land that stretched back to the higher bluffs. The house toward which the young fellow turned was painted white, and had the dark-green blinds which transplanted New-Englanders carry with them wherever they go.

Soldierly Lombardy poplar trees stood in the yard, and beds of flowers lined the walk. Mrs. Miner was at work in the beds when he came up.

"Good day," he said cordially. "Glorious spring weather, isn't it?" He smiled pleasantly. "Is this Mrs. Miner?"

"Yes, sir." She looked at him wonderingly.

"I'm one of Wilber's men," he explained. "He couldn't get away, so he sent me up to see what needed doing."

"Oh," she said, with a relieved tone. "Very well; will you go look at it?"

They walked, side by side, out toward the barn, which had the look of great age in its unpainted decay. It was gray as granite and worn fuzzy with sleet and snow. The young fellow looked around at the grass, the dandelions, the vague and beautiful shadows flung down upon the turf by the scant foliage of the willows and apple trees, and took off his hat, as if in the presence of something holy. "What a lovely place!" he said—"all but the mill down there; it seems too bad it burnt up. I hate to see a ruin, most of all, one of a mill." She looked at him in surprise, perceiving that he was not at all an ordinary carpenter. He had a thoughtful face, and the workman's dress he wore could not entirely conceal a certain delicacy of limb. His voice had a touch of cultivation in it.

"The work I want done is on the barn," she said at length. "Do you think it needs reshingling?"

He looked up at it critically, his head still bare. She was studying him carefully now, and admired his handsome profile. There was something fine and powerful in the poise of his head.

"You haven't been working for Mr. Wilber long," she said.

He turned toward her with a smile of gratification, as if he knew she had detected something out of the ordinary in him.

"No, I'm just out of Beloit," he said, with ready confidence. "You see that I'm one of these fellows who have to work my passage. I put in my vacations at my trade." He looked up at the roof again, as if checking himself. "Yes, I should think from here that it would have to be reshingled."

She sighed resignedly, and he knew she was poor. "Well, I suppose you had better do it."

She thought of him pleasantly, as he walked off down the road after the lumber and tools that were necessary. And, in his turn, he wondered whether she were a widow or not. It promised to be a pleasant job. She was quite handsome, in a serious way, he decided—very womanly and dignified. Perhaps this was his romance, he thought, with the ready imagination upon this point of a youth of twenty-one.

He returned soon with a German teamster, who helped him unload his lumber and erect his stagings. When noon came he was working away on the roof, tearing the old shingles off with a spade.

He was a little uncertain about his dinner. It was the custom

Hamlin Garland

to board carpenters when they were working on a farm, but this farm was so near town, possibly Mrs. Miner would not think it necessary. He decided, however, to wait till one o'clock, to be sure. At half past twelve, a man came in out of the field with a team—a short man, with curly hair, curly chin beard, and mustache. He walked with a little swagger, and his legs were slightly bowed. Morris called him "a little feller," and catalogued him by the slant on his hat.

"Say," called Morris suddenly, "won't you come up here and help me raise my staging?"

The man looked up with a muttered curse of surprise. "Who the hell y' take me for? Hired man?" he asked, and then, after a moment, continued, in a tone which was an insult: "You don't want to rip off the whole broad side of that roof. Ain't y' got any sense? Come a rain, it'll raise hell with my hay."

"It ain't going to rain," Morris replied. He wanted to give him a sharp reply, but concluded not to do so. This was evidently the husband. His romance was very short.

"Tom, won't you call the man in?" asked Mrs. Miner, as her husband came up to the kitchen door.

"No, call 'im yourself. You've got a gullet."

Mrs. Miner's face clouded a little, but she composed herself. "Morty, run out and tell the carpenter to come to dinner."

"Boss is in a temper," Morris thought, as he listened to Miner's reply. He came up to the well, where Morty brought him a clean towel, and waited to show him into the kitchen.

Miner was just sitting down to the table when Morris entered. His sleeves were rolled up. He had his old white hat on his head. He lounged upon one elbow on the table. His whole bearing was swinish.

"What do I care?" he growled, as if in reply to some low-voiced warning his wife had uttered. "If he don't like it, he can lump it, and if you don't like my ways," he said, turning upon her, "all you've got to do is to say so, and I git out."

Morris was amazed at all this. He could not persuade himself that he had rightly understood what had been said. There was something beneath the man's words which puzzled him and forbade his inquiry. He sat down near the oldest child and opposite Mrs. Miner. Miner began to eat, and Morris was speaking pleasantly to the child nearest him, when he heard an oath and a slap. He looked up to see Miner's hat falling from Mrs. Miner's cheek.

She had begun a silent grace, and her husband had thrown his hat in her face. She kept her eyes upon her plate, and her lips moved as if in prayer, though a flush of red streamed up her neck and covered her cheek.

Morris leaped up, his eyes burning into Miner's face. "H'yere!" he shouted, "what's all this? Did you strike her?"

"Set down!" roared Miner. "You're too fresh."

"I'll let you know how fresh I am," said the young fellow, shaking his brawny fist in Miner's face.

Mrs. Miner rose, with a ghastly smile on her face, which was now as pale as it had been flushed. "Please don't mind him; he's only fooling." Morris looked at her and understood a little of her feeling as a wife and mother. He sat down. "Well, I'll let him know the weight of my fist, if he does anything more of that business when I'm around," he said, looking at her, and then at her husband. "I didn't grow up in a family where things like that go on. If you'll just say the word, I—I'll—"

"Please don't do anything," she said, and he saw that he had better not, if he wished to shield her from further suffering. The meal proceeded in silence. Miner apparently gloried in what he had done.

The children were trembling with fear and could scarcely go on with their dinners. They dared not cry. Their eyes were fixed upon their father's face, like the eyes of kittens accustomed to violence. The wife tried to conceal her shame and indignation. She thought she succeeded very well, but the big tears rolling down from her wide unseeing eyes, were pitiful to witness.

Morris ate his dinner in silence, not seeing anything further to do or say. His food choked him, and he found it necessary to drink great draughts of water.

At last she contrived to say, "How did you find the roof?" It was a pitiful attempt to cover the dreadful silence.

"It was almost as good as no roof at all," he replied, with the desire to aid her. "Those shingles, I suppose, have been on there for thirty years. I suppose those shingles must have been rived out by just such a machine as Old Man Means used, in the 'Hoosier Schoolmaster.'" From this, he went on to tell about some of the comical parts of the story, and so managed to end the meal in a fairly presentable way.

"She's found another sympathizer," sneered the husband, returning to his habit of addressing his wife in the third person.

After eating his dinner, Miner lit his pipe and swaggered out, as if he had done an admirable thing. Morris remained at the table, talking with the children. After Miner had passed out of earshot, he looked up at Mrs. Miner, as if expecting her to say something in explanation of what had occurred. But she had again forgotten him, and sat biting her lips and looking out of the window. Her bosom heaved like that of one about to weep. Her wide-open eyes had unutterable sorrow in their beautiful depths.

Morris got up and went out, in order to prevent himself from weeping too. He hammered away on the roof like mad for an hour, and wished that every blow fell on that little villain's curly pate.

He did not see Mrs. Miner to speak to her again till the next forenoon, when she came out to see how the work was getting on. He came down from the roof to meet her, and they stood side by side, talking the job over and planning other work. She spoke, at last, in a low, hesitating voice, and without looking at him:

"You mustn't mind what Mr. Miner does. He's very peculiar, and you're likely—that is, I mean—"

She could not finish her lie. The young man looked down on her resolutely. "I'd like to lick him, and I'd do it for a leather cent."

She put out her hand with a gesture of dismay. "Oh, don't make trouble; please don't!"

"I won't if you don't want me to, but that man needs a licking the worst of any one I ever saw. Mrs. Miner," he said, after a little pause, "I wish you'd tell me why he acts that way. Now, there must be some reason for it. No sane man is going to do a thing like that."

She looked away, a hot flush rising upon her face. She felt a distinct longing for sympathy. There was something very engaging in this young man's candid manner.

"I do not know who is to blame," she said at last, as if in answer to a question. "I've tried to be a good wife to him for the children's sake. I've tried to be patient. I suppose if I'd made the property all over to him, as most wives do, at first, it would have avoided all trouble." She paused to think a moment.

"But, you see" she went on suddenly, "father never liked him at all, and he made me promise never to let the mill or the farm go out of my hands, and then I didn't think it necessary. It belonged to us both, just as much as if I'd signed it over. I considered he was my partner as well as my husband. I knew how father felt, especially about the mill, and I couldn't go against his wish."

She had the impulse to tell it all now, and she sat down on a bunch of shingles, as if to be able to state it better. Her eyes were turned away, her hands pressed upon each other like timid, living things seeking aid, and, looking at her trembling lips, the young man felt a lump rise in his throat.

"It began all at once, you see. I mean the worst of it did. Of course, we'd had sharp words, as all people who live together are apt to have, I suppose, but they didn't last long. You see, everything was mine, and he had nothing at all when he came home with me. He'd had bad luck, and he—he never was a good business man."

The tears were on her face again. She was retrospectively approaching that miserable time when her suffering began.

The droop of her head appealed to the young man with immense power. He had an impulse to take her in his arms and comfort her, as if she were his sister.

She mastered herself at last, and went on in low, hesitating voice, more touching than downright sobbing: "One day, the same summer the mill burned, one of the horses kicked at little Morty, and I said I'd sell it, and he said it was all nonsense; the horse wasn't to blame. And I told him I wouldn't have a horse around that would kick. And when he said I shouldn't sell it, I said a dreadful thing. I knew it would cut him, but I said it. I said: 'The horse is mine; the farm is mine; I can do what I please with my own, for all of you.'"

She fell silent here, and Morris was forced to ask, "What did he do then?"

"He looked at me, a queer, long look that made me shiver, and then he walked off, and he never spoke to me again directly for six months. And from that day he almost never speaks to me except through the children. He calls me names through them. He cuts me every time he can. He does everything he can to hurt me. He never dresses up, and he wears his hat in the house at all times, and rolls up his sleeves at the table, just because he knows it makes me suffer. Sometimes I think he is crazy, and yet—"

"Oh, no, he ain't crazy. He's devilish," Morris blurted out. "Great guns! I'd like to lay my hands on him."

She seemed to feel that a complete statement was demanded. "I can't invite anybody to the house, for there's no knowing what he'll do. He may stay in the fields all day and never come in at all, or he may come in and curse and swear at me or do something—I never can tell what he is goin' to do."

"Haven't you any relatives here?" Morris asked.

"Yes, but I'm ashamed to let them know about it, because they all said I'd repent; and then he's my husband, and he's the father of my children."

"A mighty poor excuse of one I call him," said the young man with decision.

"I tried to give him the farm, when I found it was going to make trouble, but he wouldn't take it *then*. He won't listen to me at all. He keeps throwing it up to me that he's earning his living, and if I don't think he is he will go any minute. He works in the field, but that's all. He won't advise with me at all. He says it's none of his business. He won't do a thing around the house or garden. I tried to get him to oversee the mill for me, but, after our trouble, he refused to do anything about it. I hired a man to run it, but it didn't pay that way, and then it was idle for a while, and at last it got afire some way and burned up—tramps, I suppose.

"Oh, dear!" she sighed, rising, "I don't see how it's going to end; it must end some time. Sometimes it seems as if I couldn't stand it another day, and then I think of my duty as a mother and wife, and I think perhaps God intended this to be my cross."

The young fellow was silent. It was a great problem. The question of divorce had never before been borne in upon him in this personal way. It seemed to him a clear case. The man ought to be driven off and the woman left in peace. He thought of the pleasure it would give her to hear the sound of the mill again.

They stood there side by side, nearly the same age, and yet the woman's face was already lined with suffering, and her eyes were full of shadow. There seemed no future for her, and yet she was young.

"Please don't let him know I've said anything to you, will you?"

"I'll try not to," he said, but he did not consider himself bound to any definite concealment.

They ate dinner together without Miner, who had a fit of work on hand which made him stubbornly unmindful of any call to eat. Moreover, he was sure it would worry his wife.

The meal was a pleasant one on the whole, and they found many things in common to talk about. Morris wanted to ask her a few more questions about her life, but she begged him not to do so, and started him off on the story of his college life. He was an enthusiastic talker and told her his plans with boyish frankness. He forgot his fatigue, and she lost for a time her premature cares and despairs. They were laughing together over some of his college pranks when Miner came in at the door.

"Oh, I see!" he said, with an insulting, insinuating inflection. "Now I understand the early dinner."

Morris sprang up and, walking over to the sneering husband, glared down at him with a look of ferocity that sat singularly upon his round, fresh face. "Now you *shut up*! If you open your mouth to me again I'll lick you till your hide won't hold pumpkins!"

Miner shrank back, turned on his heel, and went off to the barn. He did not return for his dinner.

Morris insisted on helping Mrs. Miner clear up the yard and

uncover the grapevine. He liked her very much. She appealed to the protector in him, and she interested him besides, because of the melancholy which was lined on her delicate face, and voiced in her low, soft utterances.

He appealed to her, because of his delicacy as well as strength. He had something of the modern man's love for flowers, and did not attempt to conceal his delight in thus tinkering about at woman's work. He ate supper with her and worked on until it was quite dark, tired as he was, and then shook hands and said "Good night."

Morris came back to his work the next day with a great deal of pleasure. He had spent considerable thought upon the matter. He had almost determined on a course of action. He had thought of going directly to Miner and saying:

"Now look here, Miner, if you was *half* a man, you'd pull out and leave this woman in peace. How you can stand around here and occupy the position you do, I don't see."

But when he remembered Mrs. Miner's words about the children, another consideration came in. Suppose he should take the children with him—that was the point; that was the uncertain part of the problem. It did not require any thought to remember that the law took very little consideration of the woman's feelings. He said to himself that if he ever became judge, he would certainly give decisions that would send such a man as Miner simply whirling out into space.

Miner was in the barn when Morris clambered up the ladder with a bunch of shingles on his shoulder, about seven o'clock. He came out and said:

"Say, you want to fix that window up there."

"Get away from there!" shouted Morris, in uncontrollable rage, "or I'll smash this bunch of shingles on your cursed head. Don't you open that ugly p'tater trap at me, you bow-legged little skunk! I'm goin' to lick you like a sock before I'm done with you."

He would have done so then had he been on the ground, but he disdained taking the trouble to climb down. He planned to catch him when he came up to dinner. The more he thought of it the more his indignation waxed. As he grew to hate the man more, he began to entertain the suspicions, which Wilber confessed to in confidence, concerning the burning of the mill.

They had a cheerful meal together again, for Miner did not come in until one o'clock. During the nooning Morris finished spading the flower beds, in spite of Mrs. Miner's entreaties that he should rest. It gave him great pleasure to work there with her and the children.

"You see, I'm lonesome here," he explained. "Just out of school, and I miss the boys and girls. I don't know anybody except a few of the carpenters here, and so—well, I kind of like it. I always helped around the house at home. It's all fun for me, so don't you say a word. I've got lots o' muscle to spare, and you're welcome to it."

He spaded away without many words. The warm sun shone down upon them all, and they made a pretty group. Mrs. Miner, rake in hand, was pulverizing the beds as fast as he spaded, her face flushed and almost happy. The children were wrist-deep in the fresh earth, planting twigs and pebbles, their babble of talk some way akin to the cry of the woodpecker, the laugh of the robin, the twitter of the sparrow, the smell of spring, and the merry downpour of sunshine.

Mrs. Miner was silent. She was thinking how different her life would have been if her husband had only taken an interest in her affairs. She did not think of any one else as her husband, but only Miner in a different mood.

Morris went back to work. As the work neared the end, his determination to punish the scoundrel husband grew. His inclination to charge him with burning the mill grew stronger. He wondered if it wouldn't serve as a club. "Now, sir," he said, meeting Miner as he came out of the barn that night, "I'm done on the barn, but I'm not done on you. I'm goin' to whale you till you won't know yourself. I ought 'o 'a done it that first day at dinner." He advanced upon Miner, who backed away, scared at something he saw in the young man's eyes and something he heard in his inflexible tone of voice.

He thrust out his palm in a wild gesture. "Keep away from me! I'll split your heart if you touch me!"

Morris advanced another step, his eyes looking straight into Miner's with the level look of a tiger's. "No, y' won't! You're too much of an infernal, sneaky little *whelp*!"

At the word whelp, he cuffed him with his hammerlike fist, and Miner went down in a heap. He was so abject that the young man could only strike him with his open hand.

He took him by the shirt collar with his left hand and began to cuff him leisurely and terribly with his right. His blows punctuated his sentences. "You're a little [whack] villain. I'll thrash you till you won't see out of your blasted eyes for a month! I can't stand a man [here he jounced him up and down with his left hand, apparently with infinite satisfaction] who bullies his wife and children as you do [here he cuffed him again], and I'll make it my business to even things up—"

The prostrate man began to scream for help. He was livid with fear. He fancied murder in the blaze of his assailant's eye.

"Help! help! Minnie!"

"Call her by her first name now, will yeh? will yeh? Call her out to help yeh! Do you think she will? I want to tell you, besides, I know something about that mill burning. It's just like your contemptible mustard-seed of a soul to burn that mill!"

Mrs. Miner came flying out. She could not recognize her husband in the bleeding, dirty, abject thing squirming under the young man's knee.

"Why, Mr. Morris, who—why—why, it's Tom!" she gasped, her eyes distended with surprise and horror.

Morris looked up at her coolly. "Yes, it's Tom." He then gave his attention to the writhing figure under him. "Crawl, you infernal whelp! Lick the dust, confound you! Quick!" he commanded, growing each moment more savage.

Mrs. Miner clung to his arm. "Please don't," she pleaded. "You're killing him."

Morris did not look up. "Oh, no, I ain't. I'm giving him a little taste of his own medicine." He flopped Miner over on his face and dragged him around in the dust like an old sack. "Beg her pardon, or I'll thrash the ground with yeh!"

"Please don't," pleaded the wife, using her whole strength to stop him in his circuit with the almost insensible Miner.

"Beg!" he said again, "beg, or I'll cave your backbone in."

There was a terrible upward inflection in his voice now, a half-jocular tone that was more terrible than the muffled snarl in which he had previously been speaking.

"I beg! I beg!" cried Miner.

Morris released him, and he crawled to a sitting posture. Mrs. Miner fell on her knees by his side, and began wiping the blood from his face. She was breathless with sobbing and the children were screaming. The tears streamed down her face, which was white and drawn into ghastly wrinkles.

"You've killed him!" she gasped.

Morris put his hands in his pockets and looked down on them both, with a curious feeling of having done something which he might repent of. He felt in a way cut off from the satisfactory ending of the thing he had planned.

"Oh, you've killed him!"

"Oh, no, I haven't. He's all right." He looked at them a moment longer to see if there were any rage remaining in the face of the husband, and then at the wife to discover her feeling concerning his action. Then he looked back at the husband again, and apparently justified himself for what he had done by the memory of the ineffable shame to which the wife had been subjected.

"Now, if I hear another word of your abuse," he said, as he shook the dust from his own clothes and prepared to go, "I'll give you another that will make you think that this is all fooling. More than that," he said, turning again, "I know something that will put you where the crows won't eat you!—If I can be of any service to you, Mrs. Miner, at any time while I'm here, I hope you'll let me know. Good-by."

Mrs. Miner did not reply, and when Morris reached the gate and looked back she was still kneeling by the side of her husband, the sunlight shining down upon her graceful head. Some way the problem had increased in complexity. He felt a disgust of her weakness, mingled with a feeling that he was losing something very fine and tender which had but just come into his life.

He went back to his work on the other side of the river, where his crew was working. He was called home a few weeks later, and he never saw husband or wife again. He learned from Wilber, however, in a short letter that things were going much the same as ever.

"Dear Sir: I don't know much about Miner. Hees purty quiet I guess. Dock Moss thinks hees a little off his nut. I don't. I think its pur cussidness."

Hamlin Garland

OF THOSE WHO SEEK

I

THE PRISONED SOUL

The Capitol swarmed with people.

Groups of legislators tramped noisily along the corridors, laughing loudly, gesticulating with pointed fingers or closed fists.

Squads of ragged, wondering, and wistful-eyed negroes, splashed with orange-colored mud from the fields, moved timidly on from magnificence to magnificence, keeping close to each other, solemn and silent. When they spoke they whispered. Others from the city streets laughed loudly and swaggered along to show their contempt for the place and their knowledge of its public character; but their insolence was half assumed.

Lean and lank Southerners, with the imperial cut on their pale, brown whiskers, alternated with stalwart, slouch-hatted Westerners. Clean-shaven, pale clerks hurried to and fro; groups of sightseers infested every nook, and wore the look of those determined to see it all. They were accompanied often by one whose certainty of accent gave evidence of his fitness to be their guide. The sound of his voice proclaimed his judgments as he pushed his dazed wordless victims about.

In a group in the center of the checkered marble floor of the rotunda, a powerful Indian, dressed in semi-civilized fashion, was standing, looking wonderingly down into the upturned face of a little girl. The circle of bystanders silently studied both man and maid.

She was about eleven years of age and was tastefully dressed, and seemed a healthy child. Her face was solemn, sweet, and inquisitive. She held one half-opened hand in the air; with the other she touched the Indian's dark, strongly molded cheek, and pressed his long hair which streamed from beneath his broad white hat.

No one smiled. She was deaf and dumb and blind.

In her raised rosy little palm, with lightning-swift motion, fluttered the hand of her teacher. By the teacher's side stood an Indian interpreter, dressed in hunting shirt and broad hat.

"I am Umatilla," said the chief, in answer to a question from the teacher. His deep voice was like the mutter of a lion; he stood with gentle dignity still looking wonderingly down into the girl's sweet, solemn, and eager face.

A bystander said, "Poor child!" in a low, tremulous tone, followed by a sigh.

The little one's hand, light, swift, and seeking, touched the Indian's ringed ears and pressed again his long hair, while her teacher's swift fingers said, "This strange man comes from a far-off land, from vast mountains and forests away toward the western sea. The wind and sun have made his face dark, and the long hair is a protection from the cold. He is a chief."

Under her broad hat the child's exquisite mouth, with its dimpled corners, remained calm but touchingly wistful. Her eyes were in shadow. Her chin was a perfect oval, delicately beautiful, like the curving lines of a peach, with the clear transparency of color of a flower's chalice.

But the bystander said again, "Poor child!" as if a shudder of awe, of wordless compassion and bitterness, shook him.

She was so beautiful, so gifted in spirit, to be thus shut in! Her inclosing flesh was so fine and sweet, it seemed impossible it could be an impassable, almost impenetrable wall.

He thought: She will soon be a woman, with all the vague, unutterable longings and passions of the woman. Her lithe body will be as beautiful as her soul, and the warm oval of her face will flash and flame with her expanding, struggling life. Her caged soul will struggle for light and companionship, blindly, vainly.

Life to her must remain a cruel fragment. Light and color she may not miss; but wifehood, maternity, the touch of baby lips to her breast—these her soul will grope for in dumb maternal desire. She must inhabit her dark and soundless cavern alone.

Again she touched the chieftain's hair and earrings, and let her hand drop down along his sleeve to his hard, brown hand. Then her hand fell to her side with a resigned action.

As she walked away, a sweet smile of pleasure and gratitude flashed for an instant across the exquisite curving line of her lips, and then the sad and wistful repose of her face came back again as if her loneliness had only been lightened, not warmed.

The young man drew a long breath of pain keen as a physical hurt. The elderly gentleman said again, "Poor child!"

The Indian looked up again into the mighty dome soaring hundreds of feet above him, and wondered how those forms came to be set flying in mid-air, and his heart grew sad and wistful too, as if a realization of the power and majesty of the white man fell like a poisonous, fateful shadow over his people and himself.

II

A SHELTERED ONE

The young man came in out of the cold dash of rain. The negro man received his outside garments and ushered him into the drawing-room, where a bright fire welcomed him like a smiling hostess.

He sat down with a sudden relaxation of his muscles. As he waited at his ease, his senses absorbed the light and warmth and beauty of the house. It was familiar and yet it had a new meaning to him. A bird was singing somewhere in the upper chambers, caroling with a joyous note that seemed to harmonize with the warmth and color of the room in which the caller sat.

The young man stared at the fire, his head leaning on his hand. There were lines of gloomy thought in his face. There were marks of bitter struggle on his hands. His dress was strong and good, but not in the mode. He looked like a young lawyer, with his lean, dark face, smoothly shaven save for a little tuft on either cheek. His long hands were heavy-jointed with toil.

He listened to the bird singing and to the answering, chirping call of a girl's voice. His head drooped forward in deep reverie.

How beautiful her life is! his thought was. How absolutely without care or struggle! She knows no uncertainty such as I feel daily, hourly. She has never a doubt of daily food; the question of clothes has been a diversion for her, a worry of choice merely. Dirt, grime, she knows nothing of. Here she lives, sheltered in a glow of comfort and color, while I hang by my finger-ends over a bottomless pit. She sleeps and dreams while I fight. She is never weary, while I sink into my bed each night as if it were my grave. Every hand held out to her is a willing hand—if it is paid for, it is willing, for she has no enemies even among her servants. O God! If I could only reach such a place to rest for just a year—for just a month! But such security, such rest is out of my reach. I must toil and toil, and when at last I reach a place to pause and rest, I shall be old and brutalized and deadened, and my rest will be merely—sleep.

He looked once more about the lovely room. The ocean wind tore at the windows with wolfish claws, savage to enter.

"The world howling out there is as impotent to do her harm as is that wind at the window," the young man added.

The bird's song again joined itself to the gay voice of the girl, and then he heard quick footsteps on the stairs, and as he rose to greet her the room seemed to glow like the heart of a ruby.

They clasped hands and looked into each other's eyes a moment. He saw love and admiration in her face. She saw only friendliness and some dark, unsmiling mood in his.

They sat down and talked upon the fringe of personalities which he avoided. She fancied that she saw a personal sorrow in his face and she longed to comfort him. She longed to touch his vexed forehead with her fingers.

They talked on, of late books and coming music. He noticed how clear and sweet and intelligent were her eyes. Refinement was in the folds of her dress and in the faint perfume which exhaled from her drapery. The firm flesh of her arms appealed to him like the limbs of a child so beautiful and tender!

He saw in her face something wistful, restless. He tried to ignore it, to seem unconscious of the adoration he saw there, for it pained him. It affected him as a part of the general misdirection of affection and effort in the world.

She asked him about his plans. He told her of them. He grew stern and savage as he outlined the work which he had set himself to do. His hands spread and clutched, and his teeth set together involuntarily. "It is to be a fight," he said; "but I shall win. Bribery, blackmail, the press, and all other forces are against me, but I shall win."

He rose at length to a finer mood as he sketched the plan which he hoped to set in action.

She looked at him with expanding eyes and quickened breath. A globed light each soft eye seemed to him.

He spoke more freely of the struggle outside in order to make her feel her own sweet security—here where the grime of trade and the reek of politics never came.

At last he rose to go, smiling a little as if in apology for his dark mood. He looked down at her slender body robed so daintily in gray and white; she made him feel coarse and rough.

Her eyes appealed to him, her glance was like a detaining hand. He felt it, and yet he said abruptly:

"Good night."

"You'll come to see me again!"

"Yes," he answered very simply and gravely.

And she, looking after him as he went down the street with head bent in thought, grew weak with a terrible weakness, a sort of hunger, and deep in her heart she cried out:

"Oh, the brave, splendid life *he* leads out there in the world! Oh, the big, brave world!"

She clinched her pink hand.

"Oh, this terrible, humdrum woman's life! It kills me, it smothers me. I must do something. I must be something. I can't live here in this way—useless. I must get into the world."

And looking around the cushioned, glowing, beautiful room, she thought bitterly:

"This is being a woman. O God, I want to be free of four walls! I want to struggle like that."

And then she sat down before the fire and whispered very softly, "I want to fight in the world—with him."

III

A FAIR EXILE

The train was ambling across the hot, russet plain. The wind, strong and warm and dry, sweeping up from the south, carried with it the subtle odor of September grass and gathered harvests. Out of the unfenced roads the dust arose in long lines like smoke from some hidden burning which the riven earth revealed. The fields were tenanted with thrashing crews, the men diminished by distance to pygmies, the long belt of the engine flapping and shining like a ribbon in the flaming sunlight.

The freight cars on the accommodation train jostled and rocked about and heaved up laterally, till they resembled a long line of awkward, frightened, galloping buffaloes. The one coach was scantily filled with passengers, mainly poorly clothed farmers and their families.

A young man seated well back in the coach was looking dreamily out of the window, and the conductor, a keen-eyed young fellow, after passing him several times, said in a friendly way:

"Going up to Boomtown, I imagine."

"Yes—if we ever get there."

"Oh, we'll get there. We won't have much more switching. We've only got an empty car or two to throw in at the junction."

"Well, I'm glad of that. I'm a little impatient because I've got a case coming up in court, and I'm not exactly fixed for it."

"Your name is Allen, I believe."

"Yes, J. H. Allen, of Sioux City."

"I thought so. I've heard you speak."

The young lawyer was a tall, slender, dark-eyed man, rather somber in appearance. He did not respond to the invitation in the conductor's voice.

"When do you reach the junction?"

"Next stop. We're only a few minutes late. Expect to meet friends there?"

"No; thought I'd get a lunch, that's all."

At the junction the car became pretty well filled with people. Two or three Norwegian families came clattering in, the mothers clothed in heavy shawls and cheap straw hats, the flaxen-haired children in faded cottonade and blue denims. They filled nearly half the seats. Several drummers came in, laughing loudly, bearing heavy valises. Then Allen heard above the noise the shrill but sweet voice of a girl, and caught the odor of violets as two persons passed him and took a seat just before him.

Hamlin Garland

The man he knew by sight and reputation as a very brilliant young lawyer, Edward Benson, of Heron Lake. The girl he knew instantly to be utterly alien to this land and people. She was like a tropic bird seen amid the scant foliage of northern hills. There was evidence of great care and taste in every fold of her modish dress. Her hat was simple but in the latest city fashion, and her gloves were spotless. She gave off an odor of cleanliness and beauty.

She was very young and slender. Her face was piquant but not intellectual, and scarcely beautiful. It pleased rather by its life and motion and oddity than by its beauty. She looked at her companion in a peculiar way—trustfully almost reverently—and yet with a touch of coquetry which seemed perfectly native to every turn of her body or glance of her eyes.

The young lawyer was a fine Western type of self-made man. He was tall and broad-shouldered, but walked a little stooping, like a man of fifty. He wore a long Prince Albert frock coat hanging loosely from his rather square shoulders. His white vest was a little soiled by his watch chain and his tie was disarranged.

His face was very fine and good. His eyes were gray-blue, deep and quiet but slightly smiling, as were his lips, which his golden-brown mustache shaded but did not hide. He was kept smiling in this quizzical way by the nervous chatter of the girl beside him. His profile, which was the view Allen had of him, was handsome. The strong, straight nose and abrupt forehead formed a marked contrast to the rather characterless nose and retreating forehead of the girl.

The first words that Allen distinguished out of the merry war in which they seemed engaged were spoken in the tone of pretty petulance such women use, a coquette's defense.

"You did, you did, you *did*. *Now!* You know you did. You told me that. You told me you despised girls like me."

"I said I despised women who had no object in life but dress," he replied, rather soberly.

"But you were hopping on me; you meant me, now! You can't deny it. You despise me, I know you do!" She challenged his flattery in her pouting self-depreciation.

The young man tried to stop her in her course, to change her mood, which was descending to real feeling. His low words could not be heard.

"Yes, yes, try to smooth it over, but you can't fool me any more. But I don't want you to flatter me and lie to me the way Judge Stearns did," she said, with a sudden change of manner. "I like you because you're square."

The phrase with which she ended seemed to take on a new meaning uttered by those red lips in childish pout.

"Now, why are you down on the judge? I don't see," said the man, as if she had gone back to an old attack.

"Well, if you'd seen what I have you'd understand." She turned away and looked out of the window. "Oh, this terrible country! I'd die out here in six weeks. I know I should."

The young lawyer was not to be turned aside.

"Of course I'm pleased to have you throw the judge over, and employ me, but, all the same, I think you do him an injustice. He's a good, square man."

"Square man!" she said, turning to him with a sudden fury in her eyes. "Do you call it square for a man—married, and gray-haired, too—to take up with a woman like Mrs. Shellberg? Say, do you, now?"

"Well, I don't quite believe—"

"Oh, I *lie*, do I?" she said, with another swift change to reproach. "You can't take my word for Mrs. Shellberg's visit to his office."

"But he was her lawyer."

"But you know what kind of a woman she is! She didn't need to go there every day or two, did she? What did he always receive her in his private office for? Come, now, tell me that."

"I don't know that he did," persisted the lawyer.

A sort of convulsion passed over her face, her little hands clinched, and the tears started into her eyes. Her voice was very quiet.

"You think I lie, then?"

"I think you are mistaken, just as other jealous women have—"

"You think I'm jealous, do you?"

"You act like a jeal—"

"Jealous of that gray-haired old wretch? No, sir! I—I—" She struggled to express herself. "I liked him, and I hated to lose all my faith in men. I thought he was good and honest when he prayed—Oh, I've seen him pray in church, the old hypocrite!" her fury returned at the recollection.

Her companion's face grew grave. The smile went out of his eyes, leaving them dark and sorrowful.

"I understand you now," he said, at last. She turned to look at him. "My practice in the divorce business out here has almost destroyed my faith in women. If it weren't for my wife and sister—"

She broke in eagerly: "Now I *know* you know what I mean. Sometimes I think men are—devils." She thrust this word forth, and her little face grew dark and strained. "But the judge kept me from thinking—I never loved my father; he didn't care for me; all he wanted to do was to make ten thousand barrels of beer a year and sell it; and the judge seemed like a father to me till *she* came and destroyed my faith in him."

"But—well, let Mrs. S. go. There are lots of good men and pure women in the world. It's dangerous to think there aren't—especially for a handsome young woman like you. You can't afford to keep in that kind of a mood long."

She looked at him curiously. "That's what I like about you," she said soberly. "You talk to me as if I had some sense—as if I was a human being. If you were to flatter me, now, and make love to me, I never would believe in any man again."

He smiled again in his frank, good way, and drew a picture from his pocket. It was a picture of a woman bending down over a laughing, naked child, sprawling frogwise in her lap. The woman's face was broad and intellectual and handsome. The look of splendid maternity was in her eyes. They both looked at the picture in silence. The girl sighed.

"I wish I was as good as that woman looks."

"You can be if you try."

"Not with a big Chicago brewer for a father and a husband that beats you whenever the mood takes him."

"I admit that's hard. I think the atmosphere of that Heron Lake hotel isn't any great help to you."

"Oh, they're a gay lot there! We fight like cats and dogs." A look of slyness and boldness came over her face. "Mrs. Shellberg hates me as hard as I do her. She used to go around telling, 'It's very peculiar, you know'"—she imitated her rival's voice—"'but no matter which end of the dining room I sit, all the men look that way!'"

The young lawyer laughed at her in spite of himself.

"But they don't, now. That's the reason she hates me," she said, in conclusion. "The men don't notice her when I'm around."

To hear her fresh young lips utter those words with their vile inflections was like taking a sudden glimpse into the underworld where harlots dwell and the spirits of unrestrained lusts dance in the shadowy recesses of the human heart.

Allen, hearing this fragmentary conversation, fascinated yet uneasy, looked at the pair with wonder. They seemed unconscious of their public situation.

The young lawyer looked straight before him while the girl, swept on by her ignoble rage, displayed still more of the moral ulceration which had been injected into her young life.

"I don't see what men find about her to like—unless it is her eyes. She's got beautiful eyes. But she's vulgar—ugh! The stories she tells—right before men, too! She'd kill any one that got ahead of her, that woman would! And yet she'll come into my room and cry and cry and say: 'Don't take him away from me! Leave him to me.' Ugh! It makes me sick." She stamped her foot, then added, irrelevantly: "She wears a wig, too. I suppose that old fool of a judge thinks it's her own hair."

The lawyer sat in stony silence. His grave face was accusing in its set expression, and she felt it and was spurred on to do still deeper injustice to herself—an insane perversity.

"Not that I care a cent—I'm not jealous of her. I ain't so bad off for company as she is. She can't take anybody away from me, but she must go and break down my faith in the judge."

She bit her lips to keep from crying out. She looked out of the window again, seeking control.

The "divorce colony" never appeared more sickening in its inner corruptions than when delineated by this dainty young girl. Allen could see the swarming men about the hotels; he could see their hot, leering eyes and smell their liquor-laden breaths as they named the latest addition to the colony or boasted of their associations with those already well known.

The girl turned suddenly to her companion.

"How do those people live out here on their farms?"

She pointed at a small shanty where the whole family stood to watch the train go by.

"By eating boiled potatoes and salt pork."

"Salt pork!" she echoed, as if salt pork were old boot-heels or bark or hay. "Why, it takes four hours for salt pork to digest!"

He laughed again at her childish irrelevancy. "So much the better for the poor. Where'd you learn all that, anyway?"

"At school. Oh, you needn't look so incredulous! I went to boarding school. I learned a good deal more than you think."

"Well, so I see. Now, I should have said pork digested in three hours, speaking from experience."

"Well, it don't. What do the women do out here?"

"They work like the men, only more so."

"Do they have any new things?"

"Not very often, I'm afraid."

She sighed. After a pause she said:

"You were raised on a farm?"

"Yes. In Minnesota."

"Did you do work like that?" She pointed at a thrashing machine in the field.

"Yes, I plowed and sowed and reaped and mowed. I wasn't on the farm for my health."

"You're very strong, aren't you?" she asked admiringly.

"In a slab-sided kind of a way—yes."

Her eyes grew abstracted.

"I like strong men. Ollie was a little man, not any taller than I am, but when he was drunk he was what men call a—a— holy terror. He struck me with the water pitcher once—that was just before baby was born. I wish he'd killed me." She ended in a sudden reaction to hopeless bitterness. "It would have saved me all these months of life in this terrible country."

"It might have saved you from more than you think," he said quietly, tenderly.

"What do you mean?"

"You've been brought up against women and men who have defiled you. They've made your future uncertain."

"Do you think it's so bad as that? Tell me!" she insisted, seeing his hesitation.

"You're on the road to hell!" he said, in a voice that was very low, but it reached her. It was full of pain and grave reprimand and gentleness. "You've been poisoned. You're in need of a good man's help. You need the companionship of good, earnest women instead of painted harlots."

Her voice shook painfully as she replied:

"You don't think I'm *all* bad?"

"You're not bad at all—you're simply reckless. *You* are not to blame. It depends upon yourself now, though, whether you keep a true woman or go to hell with Mrs. Shellberg."

The conductor eyed them as he passed, with an unpleasant

light in his eyes, and the drummers a few seats ahead turned to look at them. The tip had passed along from lip to lip. They were like wild beasts roused by the presence of prey. Their eyes gleamed with relentless lust. They eyed the little creature with ravening eyes. Her helplessness was their opportunity.

Allen, sitting there, saw the terror and tragedy of the girl's life. Her reckless, prodigal girlhood; the coarse, rich father; the marriage, when a thoughtless girl, with a drunken, dissolute boy; the quarrels, brutal beatings; the haste to secure a divorce; the contamination of the crowded hotels in Heron Lake—and this slender young girl, naturally pure, alert, quick of impulse—she was like a lamb among lustful wolves. His heart ached for her.

The deep, slow voice of the lawyer sounded on. His eyes turned toward her had no equivocal look. He was a brother speaking to a younger sister. The tears fell down her cheeks, upon her folded hands. Her widely opened eyes seemed to look out into a night of storms.

"Oh, what shall I do?" she moaned. "I wish I was dead—and baby too!"

"Live for the baby—let him help you out."

"Oh, he can't! I don't care enough for him. I wish I was like other mothers; but I'm not. I can't shut myself up with a baby. I'm too young."

He saw that. She was seeking the love of a man, not the care of a child. She had the wifely passion, but not the mother's love. He was silent; the case baffled him.

"Oh, I wish you could help me. I wish I had you all the time.

I do! I don't care what you think, *I do, I do!*"

"Our home is open to you and baby, too," he said slowly. "My wife knows about you, and—"

"Who told her—did you?" she flashed out again, angrily, jealously.

"Yes. My wife is my other self," he replied quietly.

She stared at him, breathing heavily, then looked out of the window again. At last she turned to him. She seemed to refer to his invitation.

"Oh, this terrible land! Oh, I couldn't stay here. I'd go insane. Perhaps I'm going insane anyway. Don't you think so?"

"No, I think you're a little nervous, that's all."

"Oh! Do you think I'll get my divorce?"

"Certainly, without question."

"Can I wait and go back with you?"

"I shall not return for several days. Perhaps you couldn't bear the wait in this little town; it's not much like the city."

"Oh, dear! But I can't go about alone. I hate these men, they stare at me so! I wish I was a man. It's awful to be a woman, don't you think so? Please don't laugh."

The young lawyer was far from laughing, but this was her only way of defending herself. These pert, birdlike ways formed her shield against ridicule and misprision.

He said slowly, "Yes, it's an awful thing to be a woman, but it's an awful responsibility to be a man."

"What do you mean?"

"I mean that we are responsible as the dominant sex for every tragic, incomplete woman's life."

"Don't you blame Mrs. Shellberg?" she said, forcing him to a concrete example with savage swiftness.

"No. She had a poor father and a poor husband, and she must earn her own living some way."

"She could cook, or nurse, or something like that."

"It isn't easy to find opportunity to cook or nurse. If it were as easy to earn a living in a pure way as it is in a vicious way all men would be rich and virtuous. But what had you planned to do after your divorce?"

"Oh, I'm going to travel for two years. Then I'll try to settle down."

"What you need is a good husband and a little cottage where you'd have to cook your own food—and tend the baby."

"I wouldn't cook for any man living," she broke in, to express her bitterness that he could so coldly dispose of her future. "Oh, this terrible train! Can't it go faster? If I'd realized what a trip this was, I wouldn't have started."

"This is the route you all go," he replied with grim humor, and his words pictured a ceaseless stream of divorcees.

She resented his classing her with the rest, but she simply

said: "You despise me, don't you? But what can we do? You can't expect us to live with men we hate, can you? That would be worse than Mrs. Shellberg."

"No, I don't expect that of you. I'd issue a divorce coupon with every marriage certificate, and done with it," he said, in desperate disgust. "Then this whole cursed business would be done away with. It isn't a question of our laxity of divorce laws," he said, after a pause, "it's a question of the senseless severity of the laws in other States. That's what throws this demoralizing business into our hands here."

"It pays, don't it? I know I've paid for everything I've had."

"Yes, that's the demoralizing thing. It draws a gang of conscienceless attorneys here, and it draws us who belong here off into dirty work, and it brings us into contact with men and women—I'm sick of the whole business."

She had hardly followed him in his generalizations. She brought him back to the personal.

"You're sick of me, I know you are!" She leaned her head on the window pane. Her eyes closed. "Oh, I wish my heart would stop beating!" she said, in a low tone.

Allen, sitting so close behind them, was forced to hear her, so piercingly sweet was her voice. He trembled for fear some one else might hear her. It seemed like profanation that any one but the woman's God should hear this outcry of a quivering, writhing soul.

She faced her companion again. "You're the only man I know, now, that I respect, and you despise me."

"No, I don't; I pity you."

Hamlin Garland

"That's worse. I want you to help me. Oh, if you could go with me, or if I could be with you!" Her gloved hands strained together in the agony of her desire.

His calm lips did not waver. He did not smile even about the eyes. He knew her cry sprang from her need of a brother, not from the passion of a woman.

"Our home is yours, just as long as you can bear the monotony of our simple lives," he said, in his quiet way, but it was deep-throated and unmistakable in its sincerity.

She laid her hand on his arm and clasped it hard, then turned away her head, and they rode in silence.

After they left the car, Allen sat with savage eyes and grimly set mouth, going over the problem again and again. He saw that young and helpless creature walking the gantlet between endless ranks of lustful, remorseless men, snatching at her in selfish, bestial desire.

It made him bitter and despairing to think that women should be helpless—that they should need some man to protect them against some other man. He cursed the laws and traditions that had kept women subordinate and trivial and deceptive and vacillating. He wished they could be raised to the level of the brutes till, like the tigress or she-wolf, they could not only defend themselves, but their young.

He tried to breathe a sigh of relief that she had gone out of his life but—he could not. It was not so easy to shake off the shadow of his responsibility. He followed her on her downward path till he saw her stretching out her hands in pitiful need to casual acquaintances—alone and without hope; still petite, still dainty in spite of all, still with flashes of wit, and then—

He shuddered. "O my God! Upon whom does the burden of guilt lie?"

* * * * *

On the night of his return he sat among his romping babes debating whether he should tell the story to his wife or not. As the little ones grew weary, the noise of the autumn wind—the lonely, woeful, moaning prairie wind—came to his ears and he shuddered. His wife observed it.

"What is it, Joe? Did you get a chill?"

"Oh, no. The wind sounds a little lonesome to-night, that's all." But he took his little girl into his arms and held her close.

IV

THE PASSING STRANGER

This was the story the mystic told:

It was about eleven o'clock of an October night. The street was one of the worst of the city, but it was Monday—one of its quiet nights.

The saloons flared floods of feverish light upon the walk, and breathed their terrible odors, like caverns leading downward into hell. Restless, loitering crowds moved to and fro, with rasping, uncertain footsteps, out of which the click of health had gone.

Policemen occasionally showed themselves menacingly, and the crowd responded to their impact by action quickened, like a python touched with a red-hot rod.

It was nearly time to close, and the barkeepers were beginning to betray signs of impatience with their most drunken customers.

A dark, tall man in cloak and fez moved slowly down the street. His face was serene but somber. In passing the window of a brilliantly lighted drinking place he stopped and looked in.

In the small stall, near the window and behind the counter, sat three women and two men. All had mugs of beer in their hands. The women were all young, and one of them was handsome. They were dressed nattily, jauntily, in modish, girlish hats, and their dainty jackets fitted closely to their slight figures.

Their liquor had just been served, and their voices were ringing with wild laughter. Their white teeth shone from their rouged faces with a mirth which met no answering smile from the strange young man without. He stood like a shadow against the pane.

The smile on the face of the youngest girl stiffened into a strange contortion. Her eyes looked straight ahead into the eyes of the stranger.

Her smile smoothed out. Her face paled; her eyes expanded with wonder till they lost their insane glitter, and grew sad and soft and dark.

"What is it, Nell?" the others asked.

She did not hear them. She seemed to listen. Her eyes seemed to see mountains—or clouds. A land like her childhood's home with the sunset light over it. Her mug fell with a crash to the table. She rose. Her hand silenced them, with beautiful finger raised:

"Listen! Don't you hear him? His eyes are calling me. It is Christ."

The others looked, but they saw only a tall figure moving away. He wore a long black cloak like a priest.

"Some foreign duffer lookin' in. Let 'im look," said one of the other girls.

"One o' them Egyptian jugglers," said another.

"What's the matter of ye, Nell? You look as if you'd seen a ghost of y'r grandmother. Set down an' drink y'r beer."

The girl brushed her hand over her eyes. "I'm going home," she said in a low voice from which all individuality had passed. Her face seemed anxious, her manner hurried.

"What's the matter, Nell? My God! Look at her eyes!—I'm going with her."

The girl put him aside with a gesture. Her look awed him.

One of the others began to laugh.

"Stop! You fool," one of the girls cried. They sat in silence as the younger girl went out, putting aside every hand stretched out to touch her. She walked like one in stupor—her face ghastly. The arch of her beautiful eyebrows was like that of Ophelia in her bitterest moment.

The others watched her go in silence.

One of them drew a sigh and said: "I'm going home, too; I don't feel well."

"I'll go with ye," one of the men said.

"Stay where you are!" said the girl sharply.

*   *   *   *   *

Once on the street, the younger girl hurried on the way the stranger had gone. His face seemed before her.

She could see it; she should always see it. It was the face of a young man. A firm chin, a strong mouth with a feminine curve in it, a face with a clear pallor that seemed foreign somehow. But the eyes—oh, the eyes!

They were deep and brown, and filled with an infinite sadness—for her. She felt it, and the knot of pain in the forehead, that was also for her. Something sweet and terrible went out from his presence. A knowledge of infinite space and infinite time and infinite compassion.

No man had ever looked at her like that. There was something divine in the penetrating power of his eyes.

Some way she knew he was not a priest, though his cloak and turban cap looked like it. He seemed like a scholar from some strange land—a man above passion, a man who knew God.

His eyes accused her and pitied her, while they called her.

No smile, no shrinking of lips into a sneer—nothing but pity and wonder, and something else—

And a voice seemed to say: "You are too good to be there. Follow me."

As she thought of him he seemed to stand on an immeasurable height looking down at her.

She had laughed at him—O God!—she flushed hot with shame from head to foot—but his eyes had not changed. His lips had kept their pitying droop, and his somber eyes had burned deep into the sacred places of her thought, where something sweet and girlish lay, unwasted and untrampled.

"He called me. He called me."

*   *   *   *   *

Under the trees where the moonlight threw tracing of shadows she came upon him standing, waiting for her. She held out her hand to him like a babe. He was taller than she thought.

He took her hands silently and she grew calm at once. All shame left her. She forgot her city life; she remembered only the sweet, merry life of the village where she was born. The sound of sleigh bells and song, and the lisp of wind in the grass, and songs of birds in the maples came to her.

His voice began softly:

"You are too good and sweet to be so devoured of beasts. In your little Northern home they are waiting for you. To-morrow you will go back to them."

He placed his hand, which was soft and warm and broad, over her eyes. His voice was like velvet, soft yet elastic.

"When you wake you will hate what you have been. No power can keep you here. You will go back to the simple life from which you should never have departed. You will love simple things and the pleasures of your native place."

Her face was turned upward, but her eyelids had fallen.

"When you wake you will not remember your life here. You will be a girl again, unstained and ready to begin life without remorse and without accusing memory. When I leave you at your door to-night, you will belong to the kingdom of good and not to the kingdom of evil."

He dropped her hands and pointed across the park.

"Now go to that gray house. Ring the bell, and you will be housed for the night. *Remember you are mine.* When the bell rings you will 'wake.'"

She moved away without looking back—moved mechanically like one still in sleep.

The man watched her until the door opened and admitted her; then he passed on into the shadow of the narrow street.

And this the listener gravely asked:

"One was chosen, the other left. Were the others less in need of grace?"

BEFORE THE LOW GREEN DOOR

Matilda Bent was dying; there was no doubt of that now, if there had been before. The gruff old physician—one of the many overworked and underpaid country doctors—shook his head and pushed by Joe Bent, her husband, as he passed through the room which served as dining room, sitting room, and parlor. The poor fellow slouched back to his chair by the stove as if dazed, and before he could speak again the doctor was gone.

Mrs. Ridings was just coming up the walk as the doctor stepped out of the door.

"O doctor, how is she?"

"She is a dying woman, madam."

"Oh! don't say that, doctor. What's the matter?"

"Cancer."

"Then the news was true—"

"I don't know anything of the news, Mrs. Ridings, but Mrs. Bent is dying from the effects of a cancer primarily, which she has had for years—since her last child, which died in infancy, you remember."

"But, doctor, she never told me—"

"Neither did she tell me. But no matter now. I have done all I can for her. If you can make death any easier for her, go and do it. You will find some opiate powders there with directions. Keep the pain down at all hazards. Don't let her suffer; that is useless. She is likely to last a day or two—but if any change comes to-night, send for me."

When the good matron entered the dowdy, suffocating little room where Matilda Bent lay gasping for breath, she was sick for a moment with sympathetic pain. There the dying woman lay, her world narrowed to four close walls, propped up on the pillows near the one little window. Her eyes seemed very large and bright, and the brow, made prominent by the sinking away of the cheeks, gave evidence that it was an uncommon woman who lay there quietly waiting the death angel.

She smiled, and lifted her eyebrows in a ghastly way.

"O Marthy!" she breathed.

"Matildy, I didn't know you was so bad, or I'd 'a' come before. Why didn't you let me know?" said Mrs. Ridings, kneeling by the bed and taking the ghostly hands of the sufferer in her own warm and soft palms. She shuddered as she kissed the thin lips.

"I think you'll soon be around agin," she added, in the customary mockery of an attempt at cheer. The other woman started slightly, turned her head, and gazed on her old friend long and intently. The hollowness of her neighbor's words stung her.

"I hope not, Marthy—I'm ready to go. I want to go. I don't care to live."

The two women communed by looking for a long time in each other's eyes, as if to get at the very secretest desires and hopes of the heart. Tears fell from Martha's eyes upon the cold and nerveless hands of her friend—poor, faithful hands, hacked and knotted and worn by thirty years of ceaseless daily toil. They lay there motionless upon the coverlet, pathetic protest for all the world to see.

"O Matildy, I wish I could do something for you! I want to help you so. I feel so bad that I didn't come before. Ain't they somethin'?"

"Yes, Marthy—jest set there—till I die—it won't be long," whispered the pale lips. The sufferer, as usual, was calmer than her visitor, and her eyes were thoughtful.

"I will! I will! But oh! must you go? Can't somethin' be done. Don't yo' want the minister to be sent for?"

"No, I'm all ready. I ain't afraid to die. I ain't worth savin' now. O Marthy! I never thought I'd come to this—did you? I never thought I'd die—so early in life—and die—unsatisfied."

She lifted her head a little as she gasped out these words with an intensity of utterance that thrilled her hearer—a powerful, penetrating earnestness that burned like fire.

"Are you satisfied?" pursued the steady lips. "My life's a failure, Marthy—I've known it all along—all but my children. O Marthy, what'll become o' them? This is a hard world."

The amazed Martha could only chafe the hands, and note sorrowfully the frightful changes in the face of her friend. The weirdly calm, slow voice began to shake a little.

"I'm dyin', Marthy, without ever gittin' to the sunny place we girls—used to think—we'd git to, by an' by. I've been a-gittin' deeper 'n' deeper—in the shade—till it's most dark. They ain't been no rest—n'r hope f'r me, Marthy—none. I ain't—"

"There, there! Tillie, don't talk so—don't, dear. Try to think how bright it'll be over there—"

"I don't know nawthin' about over there; I'm talkin' about here. I ain't had no chance here, Marthy."

"He will heal all your care—"

"He can't wipe out my sufferin's here."

"Yes, He can, and He will. He can wipe away every tear and heal every wound."

"No—he—can't. God himself can't wipe out what has been. O Mattie, if I was only there!—in the past—if I was only young and purty agin! You know how tall I was! how we used to run—O Mattie, if I was only there! The world was all bright then—wasn't it? We didn't expect—to work all our days. Life looked like a meadow, full of daisies and pinks, and the nicest ones and the sweetest birds was just a little ways on—where the sun was—it didn't look—wasn't we happy?"

"Yes, yes, dear. But you mustn't talk so much." The good woman thought Matilda's mind was wandering. "Don't you want some med'cine? Ain't your fever risin'?"

"But the daisies and pinks all turned to weeds," she went on, waiting a little, "when we picked 'em. An' the sunny place—has been always behind me, and the dark before me. Oh! if I was only there—in the sun—where the pinks and daisies are!"

"You mustn't talk so, Mattie! Think about your children. You ain't sorry y' had them. They've been a comfort to y'. You ain't sorry you had 'em."

"I ain't glad," was the unhesitating reply of the failing woman; and then she went on, in growing excitement: "They'll haf to grow old jest as I have—git bent and gray, an' die. They ain't ben much comfort to me; the boys are like their father, and Julyie's weak. They ain't no happiness—for such as me and them."

She paused for breath, and Mrs. Ridings, not knowing what to say, did better than speak. She fell to stroking the poor face, and the hands getting more restless each moment. It was as if Matilda Fletcher had been silent so long, had borne so much without complaint, that now it burst from her in a torrent not to be stayed. All her most secret doubts and her sweetest hopes seemed trembling on her lips or surging in her brain, racking her poor, emaciated frame for utterance. Now that death was sure, she was determined to rid her bosom of its perilous stuff. Martha was appalled.

"I used to think—that when I got married I'd be perfectly happy—but I never have been happy sence. It was the beginning of trouble to me. I never found things better than they looked; they was always worse. I've gone further an' further from the sunshiny meadow, an' the birds an' flowers—and I'll never git back to 'em again, never!" She ended with a sob and a low wail.

Her face was horrifying with its intensity of pathetic regret. Her straining, wide-open eyes seemed to be seeing those sunny spots in the meadow.

"Mattie, sometimes when I'm asleep I think I am back there ag'in—and you girls are there—an' we're pullin' off the leaves of the wild sunflower—'rich man, poor man, beggar man'—and I hear you all laugh when I pull off the last leaf; an' when I come to myself—and I'm an old, dried-up woman, dyin' unsatisfied!"

"I've felt that way a little myself, Matildy," confessed the watcher in a scared whisper.

"I knew it, Mattie; I knew you'd know how I felt. Things have been better for you. You ain't had to live in an old log house all your life, an' work yourself to skin an' bone for a man you don't respect nor like."

"Matildy Bent, take that back! Take it back, for mercy sake! Don't you dare die thinkin' that—don't you dare!"

Bent, hearing her voice rising, came to the door, and the wife, knowing his step, cried:

"Don't let him in! Don't! I can't bear him—keep him out; I don't want to see him ag'in."

"Who do you mean? Not Joe?"

"Yes. Him."

Had the dying woman confessed to murder, good Martha could not have been more shocked. She could not understand this terrible revulsion in feeling, for she herself had been absolutely loyal to her husband through all the trials which had come upon them.

But she met Bent at the threshold, and, closing the door, went out with him into the summer kitchen, where the rest of the family were sitting. A gloomy silence fell on them all after the greetings were over. The men were smoking; all were seated in chairs tipped back against the wall. Joe Bent, a smallish man, with a weak, good-natured face, asked in a hoarse whisper:

"How is she, Mis' Ridings?"

"She seems quite strong, Mr. Bent. I think you had all better go to bed; if I want you I can call you. Doctor give me directions."

"All right," responded the relieved man. "I'll sleep on the lounge in the other room. If you want me, just rap on the door."

When, after making other arrangements, Martha went back to the bedroom, she was startled to hear the sick woman muttering to herself, or perhaps because she had forgotten Martha's absence.

"But the shadows on the meadow didn't stay; they passed on, and then the sun was all the brighter on the flowers. We used to string sweet-williams on spears of grass—don't you remember?"

Martha gave her a drink of the opiate in the glass, adjusted her on the pillow, and threw open the window, even to the point of removing the screen, and the gibbous moon flooded the room with light. She did not light a lamp, for its flame would heat the room. Besides, the moonlight was sufficient. It fell on the face of the sick woman, till she looked like a thing of marble—all but her dark eyes.

"Does the moon hurt you, Tilly? Shall I put down the curtain?"

The woman heard with difficulty, and when the question was repeated said slowly:

"No, I like it." After a little—"Don't you remember, Mattie 'how beautiful the moonlight seemed? It seemed to promise happiness—and love—but it never come for us. It makes me dream of the past now—just as it did o' future then; an' the whip-poor-wills too—"

The night was perfectly beautiful, such a night as makes dying an infinite sorrow. The summer was at its liberalest. Innumerable insects of the nocturnal sort were singing in unison with the frogs in the pools. A whip-poor-will called, and its neighbor answered it like an echo. The leaves of the trees, glossy from the late rain, moved musically to the light west wind, and the exquisite perfume of many flowers came in on the breeze.

When the failing woman sank into silence, Martha leaned her elbow on the window sill, and, gazing far into the great deeps of space, gave herself up to unwonted musings upon the problems of human life. She sighed deeply at times. She found herself at moments in the almost terrifying position of a human soul in space. Not a wife, not a mother, but just a soul facing the questions which harass philosophers. As she realized her condition of mind she apprehended something of the thinking of the woman on the bed. Matilda had gone beyond or far back of the wife and mother.

The hours wore on; the dying woman stirred uneasily now and then, whispering a word or phrase which related to her girlhood—never to her later life. Once she said:

"Mother, hold me. I'm so tired."

Martha took the thin form in her arms, and, laying her head close beside the sunken cheek, sang, in half breath, a lullaby till the sufferer grew quiet again.

The eastern moon passed over the house, leaving the room dark, and still the patient watcher sat beside the bed, listening to the slow breathing of the dying one. The cool air grew almost chill; the east began to lighten, and with the coming light the tide of life sank in the dying body. The head, hitherto restlessly turning, ceased to move. The eyes grew quiet and began to soften like a sleeper's.

"How are you now, dear?" asked the watcher several times, bending over the bed, and bathing back the straying hair.

"I'm tired—tired, mother—turn me," she murmured drowsily, with heavy lids drooping.

Martha adjusted the pillows again, and turned the face to the wall. The poor, tortured, restless brain slowly stopped its grinding whirl, and the thin limbs, heavy with years of hopeless toil, straightened out in an endless sleep.

Matilda Fletcher had found rest.

UPON IMPULSE

The seminary buildings stood not far from the low, lodgelike railway station, and a path led through a gap in the fence across the meadow. People were soberly converging toward its central building, as if proceeding to church.

Among the people who alighted from the two o'clock train were Professor Blakesly and his wife and a tall, dark man whom they called Ware.

Mrs. Blakesly was plump and pretty, plainly the mother of two or three children and the sovereign of a modest suburban cottage. Blakesly was as evidently a teacher; even the casual glances of the other visitors might discover the character of these people.

Ware was not so easy to be read. His face was lean and brown, and his squarely clipped mustache gave him a stern look. His body was well rounded with muscle, and he walked alertly; his manner was direct and vigorous, manifestly of the open air.

As they entered the meadow he paused and said with humorous irresolution, "I don't know what I am out here for."

"To see the pretty girls, of course," said Mrs. Blakesly.

"They may be plain, after all," he said.

"They're always pretty at graduation time and at marriage," Blakesly interpreted.

"Then there's the ice cream and cake," Mrs. Blakesly added.

"Where do all these people come from?" Ware asked, looking about. "It's all farm land here."

"They are the fathers, mothers, and brothers of the seminary girls. They come from everywhere. See the dear creatures about the door! Let's hurry along."

"They do not interest me. I take off my hat to the beauty of the day, however."

Ware had evidently come under protest, for he lingered in the daisied grass which was dappled with shadows and tinkling with bobolinks and catbirds.

A broad path led up to the central building, whose double doors were swung wide with most hospitable intent. Ware ascended the steps behind his friends, a bored look on his dark face.

Two rows of flushed, excited girls with two teachers at their head stood flanking the doorway to receive the visitors, who streamed steadily into the wide, cool hall.

Mrs. Blakesly took Ware in hand. "Mr. Ware, this is Miss Powell. Miss Powell, this is Mr. Jenkin Ware, lawyer and friend to the Blakeslys."

"I'm very glad to see you," said a cool voice, in which gladness was entirely absent.

Ware turned to shake hands mechanically, but something in the steady eyes and clasp of the hand held out turned his listless manner into surprise and confusion. He stared at her without speaking, only for a second, and yet so long she colored and withdrew her hand sharply.

"I beg your pardon, I didn't get the name."

"Miss Powell," answered Mrs. Blakesly, who had certainly missed this little comedy, which would have been so delicious to her.

Ware moved on, shaking hands with the other teachers and bowing to the girls. He seized an early moment to turn and look back at Miss Powell. His listless indifference was gone. She was a fine figure of a woman—a strong, lithe figure, dressed in a well-ordered, light-colored gown. Her head was girlish, with a fluff of brown hair knotted low at the back. Her profile was magnificent. The head had the intellectual poise, but the proud bosom and strong body added another quality. "She is a modern type," Ware said, remembering a painting of such a head he had seen in a recent exhibition.

As he studied her she turned and caught him looking, and he felt again a curious fluttering rush at his heart. He fancied she flushed a little deeper as she turned away.

As for him, it had been a very long while since he had felt that singular weakness in the presence of a young woman. He walked on, trying to account for it. It made him feel very boyish. He had a furtive desire to remain in the hall where he could watch her, and when he passed up the stairs, it was with a distinct feeling of melancholy, as if he were leaving something very dear and leaving it forever.

He wondered where this feeling came from, and he looked into the upturned faces of the girls as if they were pansies. He wandered about the rooms with the Blakeslys, being bored by introductions, until at last Miss Powell came up the stairway with the last of the guests.

While the girls sang and went through some pretty drills Ware again studied Miss Powell. Her appeal to his imagination was startling. He searched for the cause of it. It could not be in her beauty. Certainly she was fine and womanly and of splendid physique, but all about her were lovely girls of daintier flesh and warmer color. He reasoned that her power was in her eyes, steady, frank as sunlight, clear as water in a mountain brook. She seemed unconscious of his scrutiny.

At last they began moving down the stairs and on to the other buildings. Ware and Blakesly waited for the ladies to come down. And when they came they were in the midst of a flood of girls, and Ware had no chance to speak to them. As they moved across the grass he fell in behind Mrs. Blakesly, who seemed to be telling secrets to Miss Powell, who flushed and shook her head.

Mrs. Blakesly turned and saw Ware close behind her, and said, "O Mr. Ware, where is my dear, dear husband?"

"Back in the swirl," Ware replied.

Mrs. Blakesly artfully dropped Miss Powell's arm and fell back. "I must not desert the poor dear." As she passed Ware she said, "Take my place."

"With pleasure," he replied, and walked on after Miss

Powell, who seemed not to care to wait.

How simply she was dressed! She moved like an athlete, without effort and without constraint. As he walked quickly to overtake her a finer light fell over the hills and a fresher green came into the grass. The daisies nodding in the wind blurred together in a dance of light and loveliness which moved him like a song.

"How beautiful everything is to-day!" he said, as he stepped to her side. He felt as if he had said, "How beautiful you are!"

She flashed a quick, inquiring glance at him.

"Yes; June can be beautiful with us. Still, there is a beauty more mature, when the sickle is about to be thrust into the grain."

He did not hear what she said. He was thinking of the power that lay in the oval of her face, in the fluffy tangle of her hair. *Ah! now he knew.* With that upward glance she brought back his boy love, his teacher whom he had worshiped as boys sometimes will, with a love as pure as winter starlight. Yes, now it was clear. There was the same flex of the splendid waist, the same slow lift of the head, and steady, beautiful eyes.

As she talked, he was a youth of seventeen, he was lying at his teacher's feet by the river while she read wonderful love stories. There were others there, but they did not count. Then the tears blurred his eyes; he remembered walking behind her dead body as it was borne to the hillside burying ground, and all the world was desolate for him.

He became aware that Miss Powell was looking at him with

startled eyes. He hastened to apologize and explain. "Pardon me; you look so much like a schoolboy idol—I—I seem to see her again. I didn't hear what you said, you brought the past back so poignantly."

There was something in his voice which touched her, but before he could go on they were joined by Mr. and Mrs. Blakesly and one of the other teachers. There was a dancing light in Mrs. Blakesly's eyes as she looked at Ware. She had just been saying to her husband: "What a splendid figure Miss Powell is! How well they look together! Wouldn't it be splendid if—"

"Oh, my dear, you're too bad. Please don't match-make any more to-day. Let Nature attend to these things," Mr. Blakesly replied with manifest impatience; "Nature attended to our case."

"I have no faith in Nature any more. I want to have at least a finger in the pie myself. Nature don't work in all cases. I'm afraid Nature can't in his case."

"Careful! He'll hear you, my dear."

"Where do we go now, Miss Powell?" asked Blakesly as they came to a halt on the opposite side of the campus.

"I think they are all going to the gymnasium building. Won't you come? That is my dominion."

They answered by moving off, Mrs. Blakesly taking Miss Powell's arm. As they streamed away in files she said: "Isn't he good-looking? We've known him for years. He's all right," she said significantly, and squeezed Miss Powell's arm.

"Well, Lou Blakesly, you're the same old irrepressible!"

"Blushing already, you *dear*! I tell you he's splendid. I wish he'd take to you," and she gave Miss Powell another squeeze. "It would be *such* a match! Brains and beauty, too."

"Oh, hush!"

They entered the cool, wide hall of the gymnasium, with its red brick walls, its polished floor, and the yellow-red wooden beams lining the ceiling.

There were only a few people remaining in the hall, most of them having passed on into the museum. As they came to the various appliances, Miss Powell explained them.

"What are these things for?" inquired Mrs. Blakesly, pointing at the row of iron rings depending from long ropes.

"They are for swinging on," and she leaped lightly upward and caught and swung by one hand.

"Mercy! Do you do that?"

"She seems to be doing it now," Blakesly said.

"I am one of the teachers," Miss Powell replied, dropping to the floor.

It was glorious to see how easily she seized a heavy dumb-bell and swung it above her head. The front line of her body was majestic as she stood thus.

"Gracious! I couldn't do that," exclaimed Mrs. Blakesly.

"No, not with your style of dress," replied her husband.—"I have to pin her hat on this year," he said to Ware.

"I love it," said Miss Powell, as she drew a heavy weight from the floor and stood with the cord across her shoulder. "It adds so much to life! It gives what Browning calls the wild joy of living. Do you know, few women know what that means? It's been denied us. Only the men have known

"'The wild joys of living! the leaping from rock up to rock,
The strong rending of boughs from the fir tree, the cool silver shock
Of a plunge in the pool's living water.'

I try to teach my girls 'How good is man's life, the mere living!'"

The men cheered as she paused for a moment flushed and breathless.

She went on: "We women have been shut out from the sports too long—I mean sports in the sun. The men have had the best of it. All the swimming, all the boating, wheeling, all the grand, wild life; now we're going to have a part."

The young ladies clustered about with flushed, excited faces while their teacher planted her flag and claimed new territory for women.

Miss Powell herself grew conscious, and flushed and paused abruptly.

Mrs. Blakesly effervesced in admiring astonishment. "Well, well! I didn't know you could make a speech."

"I didn't mean to do so," she replied.

"Go on! Go on!" everybody called out, but she turned away

to show some other apparatus.

"Wasn't she fine?" exclaimed Mrs. Blakesly to Ware.

"Beyond praise," he replied. She went at once to communicate her morsel of news to her husband, and at length to Miss Powell.

The company passed out into other rooms until no one was left but Mrs. Blakesly, the professor, and Ware. Miss Powell was talking again, and to Ware mainly. Ware was thoughtful, Miss Powell radiant.

"I didn't know what life was till I could do that." She took up a large dumb-bell and, extending it at arm's length, whirled it back and forth. Her forearm, white and smooth, swelled into strong action, and her supple hands had the unwavering power and pressure of an athlete, and withal Ware thought: "She is feminine. Her physical power has not coarsened her; it has enlarged her life, but left her entirely womanly."

In some adroit way Mrs. Blakesly got her husband out of the room and left Ware and Miss Powell together. She was showing him the view from the windows, and they seemed to be perfectly absorbed. She looked around once and saw that Mrs. Blakesly was showing her husband something in the farther end of the room. After that she did not think of them.

The sun went lower in the sky and flamed along the sward. He spoke of the mystical power of the waving daisies and the glowing greens which no painter ever seems to paint. While they looked from the windows their arms touched, and they both tried to ignore it. She shivered a little as if a cold wind had blown upon her. At last she led the way out and down the stairs to the campus. They heard the gay laughter of the company at their cakes and ices, up at the central building.

He stopped outside the hallway, and as she looked up inquiringly at him, he said quietly: "Suppose we go down the road. It seems pleasanter there."

She acquiesced like one in a pleasure which made duty seem absurd.

Strong and fine as she was, she had never found a lover to whom she yielded her companionship with unalloyed delight. She was thirty years of age, and her girlhood was past. She looked at this man, and a suffocating band seemed to encircle her throat. She knew he was strong and good. He was a little saddened with life—that she read in his deep-set eyes and unsmiling lips.

The road led toward the river, and as they left the campus they entered a lane shaded by natural oaks. He talked on slowly. He asked her what her plans were.

"To teach and to live," she said. Her enthusiasm for the work seemed entirely gone.

Once he said, "This is the finest hour of my life."

On the bank of the river they paused and seated themselves on the sward under a tree whose roots fingered the stream with knuckled hands.

"Yes, every time you look up at me you bring back my boyish idol," he went on. "She was older than I. It is as if I had grown older and she had not, and that she were you, or you were she. I can't tell you how it has affected me. Every movement you make goes deep down into my sweetest, tenderest recollections. It's always June there, always sweet and sunny. Her death and burial were mystical in their beauty. I looked in her coffin. She was the grandest statue that ever lay in marble; the Greek types are insipid beside that vision. You'll say I idealized her; possibly I did, but there she is. O God! it was terrible to see one die so young and so lovely."

There was a silence. Tears came to her eyes. He could only exclaim; weeping was denied him. His voice trembled, but grew firmer as he went on:

"And now you come. I don't know exactly in what way you resemble her. I only know you shake me as no other human being has done since that coffin-lid shut out her face." He lifted his head and looked around. "But Nature is beautiful and full of light and buoyancy. I am not going to make you sad. I want to make you happy. I was only a boy to her. She cared for me only as a mature woman likes an apt pupil, but she made all Nature radiant for me, as you do now."

He smiled upon her suddenly. His somber mood passed like one of the shadows of the clouds floating over the campus. It was only a recollected mood. As he looked at her the old hunger came into his heart, but the buoyancy and emotional exaltation of youth came back also.

"Miss Powell, are you free to marry me?" he said suddenly.

She grew very still, but she flushed and then she turned her face away from him. She had no immediate reply.

"That is an extraordinary thing to ask you, I know," he went on; "but it seems as if I had known you a long time, and then sitting here in the midst of Nature with the insects singing all about us—well, conventions are not so vital as in drawing rooms. Remember your Browning."

She who had declaimed Browning so blithely now sat silent,

but the color went out of her face, and she listened to the multitudinous stir and chirp of living things, and her eyes dreamed as he went on steadily, his eyes studying her face.

"Browning believed in these impulses. I'll admit I never have. I've always reasoned upon things, at least since I became a man. It has brought me little, and I'm much disposed to try the virtue of an impulse. I feel as certain that we can be happy together as I am of life, so I come back to my question, Are you free to marry me?"

She flushed again. "I have no other ties, if that is what you mean."

"That is what I mean precisely. I felt that you were free, like myself. I might ask Blakesly to vouch for me, but I prefer not. I ask for no one's opinion of you. Can't you trust to that insight of which women are supposed to be happily possessed?"

She smiled a little. "I never boasted of any divining power."

He came nearer. "Come, you and I have gone by rule and reason long enough. Here we have a magnificent impulse; let us follow. Don't ask me to wait, that would spoil it all; considerations would come in."

"Ought they not to come in?"

"No," he replied, and his low voice had the intensity of a trumpet. "If this magnificent moment passes by, this chance for a pure impulsive choice, it is lost forever. You know Browning makes much of such lost opportunities. Seeing you there with bent head and blowing hair, I would throw the world away to become the blade of grass you break. There, will that do?" He smiled.

"That speech should bring back youth to us both," she said.

"Right action *now* will," he quickly answered.

"But I must consider."

"Do not. Take the impulse."

"It may be wayward."

"We've both got beyond the wayward impulse. This impulse rises from the profound deeps. Come, the sun sinks, the insect voices thicken, a star passes behind the moon, and life hastens. Come into my life. Can't you trust me?"

She grew very white, but a look of exaltation came into her face. She lifted her clear, steady eyes to his. She reached her hand to his. "I will," she said, and they rose and stood together thus.

He uncovered his head. A sort of awe fell upon him. A splendid human life was put into his keeping.

"A pure choice," he said exultingly—"a choice untouched by considerations. It brings back the youth of the world."

The sun lay along the sward in level lines, the sky was full of clouds sailing in file, like mighty purple cranes in saffron seas of flame, the wind wavered among the leaves, and the insects sang in sudden ecstasy of life.

The two looked into each other's faces. They seemed to be transfigured, each to the other.

"You must not go back," he said. "They would not understand you nor me. We will never be so near a great happiness, a great holiday. It is holiday time. Let us go to the mountains."

She drew a sigh as if all her cares and duties dropped from her, then she smiled and a comprehending light sparkled in her eyes.

"Very well, to the clouds if you will."

THE END OF LOVE IS LOVE OF LOVE

They lay on the cliff where the warm sun fell. Beneath them were rocks, lichen-spotted above, and orange and russet and pink beneath.

Around the headland the ocean ravened with roaring breath, flinging itself ceaselessly on the land, only to fall back with clutching snarl over the pebbles.

The smell of hot cedars was in the air. The distant ships drove by with huge sails bellying. Occasional crickets chirped faintly. Sandpipers skimmed the beach.

The man and woman were both gray. He lay staring at the sky. She sat with somber eyes fixed on the distant sea, whose crawling lines glittered in ever-changing designs on its purple sweep.

They were man and wife; both were older than their years. They were far past the land of youth and love.

"O wife!" he cried, "let us forget we are old; let us forget we are disillusioned of life; let us try to be boy and girl again."

The woman shivered with a powerful, vague emotion, but

Hamlin Garland

she did not look at him.

"O Esther, I'm tired of life!" the man went on. "I'm tired of my children. I'm tired of you. Do you know what I mean?"

The woman looked into his eyes a moment, and said in a low voice:

"No, Charles." But the man knew she meant yes. The touch of her hand grew cold.

"I'm tired of it all. I want to feel again the wonder and mystery of life. It's all gone. The love we have now is good and sweet and true; that of the old time was sweeter. It was so marvelous. I trembled when I kissed you, dear. I don't now. It had more of truth, of pure, unconscious passion, and less of habit. Oh, teach me to forget!"

He crept nearer to her, and laid his head in her lap. His face was knotted with his passion and pain.

The wife and mother sighed, and looked down at his hair, which was getting white.

"Well, Charles!" she said, and caressingly buried her fingers in his hair. "I'll try to forget for your sake."

He could not understand her. He did not try. He lay with closed eyes, tired, purposeless. The sweet sea wind touched his cheek, white with the indoor pallor of the desk worker. The sound of the sea exalted him. The beautiful clouds above him carried him back to boyhood. There were tears on his face as he looked up at her.

"I'm forgetting!" he said, with a smile of exultation.

But the woman looked away at the violet-shadowed sails, afar on the changeful purple of the sea, and her throat choked with pain.

Hamlin Garland

Choose from Thousands of 1stWorldLibrary Classics By

A. M. Barnard
Ada Leverson
Adolphus William Ward
Aesop
Agatha Christie
Alexander Aaronsohn
Alexander Kielland
Alexandre Dumas
Alfred Gatty
Alfred Ollivant
Alice Duer Miller
Alice Turner Curtis
Alice Dunbar
Allen Chapman
Alleyne Ireland
Ambrose Bierce
Amelia E. Barr
Amory H. Bradford
Andrew Lang
Andrew McFarland Davis
Andy Adams
Angela Brazil
Anna Alice Chapin
Anna Sewell
Annie Besant
Annie Hamilton Donnell
Annie Payson Call
Annie Roe Carr
Annonaymous
Anton Chekhov
Archibald Lee Fletcher
Arnold Bennett
Arthur C. Benson
Arthur Conan Doyle
Arthur M. Winfield
Arthur Ransome
Arthur Schnitzler
Arthur Train
Atticus
B.H. Baden-Powell
B. M. Bower
B. C. Chatterjee
Baroness Emmuska Orczy
Baroness Orczy
Basil King
Bayard Taylor
Ben Macomber
Bertha Muzzy Bower
Bjornstjerne Bjornson

Booth Tarkington
Boyd Cable
Bram Stoker
C. Collodi
C. E. Orr
C. M. Ingleby
Carolyn Wells
Catherine Parr Traill
Charles A. Eastman
Charles Amory Beach
Charles Dickens
Charles Dudley Warner
Charles Farrar Browne
Charles Ives
Charles Kingsley
Charles Klein
Charles Hanson Towne
Charles Lathrop Pack
Charles Romyn Dake
Charles Whibley
Charles Willing Beale
Charlotte M. Braeme
Charlotte M. Yonge
Charlotte Perkins Stetson
Clair W. Hayes
Clarence Day Jr.
Clarence E. Mulford
Clemence Housman
Confucius
Coningsby Dawson
Cornelis DeWitt Wilcox
Cyril Burleigh
D. H. Lawrence
Daniel Defoe
David Garnett
Dinah Craik
Don Carlos Janes
Donald Keyhoe
Dorothy Kilner
Dougan Clark
Douglas Fairbanks
E. Nesbit
E. P. Roe
E. Phillips Oppenheim
E. S. Brooks
Earl Barnes
Edgar Rice Burroughs
Edith Van Dyne
Edith Wharton

Edward Everett Hale
Edward J. O'Biren
Edward S. Ellis
Edwin L. Arnold
Eleanor Atkins
Eleanor Hallowell Abbott
Eliot Gregory
Elizabeth Gaskell
Elizabeth McCracken
Elizabeth Von Arnim
Ellem Key
Emerson Hough
Emilie F. Carlen
Emily Bronte
Emily Dickinson
Enid Bagnold
Enilor Macartney Lane
Erasmus W. Jones
Ernie Howard Pie
Ethel May Dell
Ethel Turner
Ethel Watts Mumford
Eugene Sue
Eugenie Foa
Eugene Wood
Eustace Hale Ball
Evelyn Everett-green
Everard Cotes
F. H. Cheley
F. J. Cross
F. Marion Crawford
Fannie E. Newberry
Federick Austin Ogg
Ferdinand Ossendowski
Fergus Hume
Florence A. Kilpatrick
Fremont B. Deering
Francis Bacon
Francis Darwin
Frances Hodgson Burnett
Frances Parkinson Keyes
Frank Gee Patchin
Frank Harris
Frank Jewett Mather
Frank L. Packard
Frank V. Webster
Frederic Stewart Isham
Frederick Trevor Hill
Frederick Winslow Taylor

L. Frank Baum
Latta Griswold
Laura Dent Crane
Laura Lee Hope
Laurence Housman
Lawrence Beasley
Leo Tolstoy
Leonid Andreyev
Lewis Carroll
Lewis Sperry Chafer
Lilian Bell
Lloyd Osbourne
Louis Hughes
Louis Joseph Vance
Louis Tracy
Louisa May Alcott
Lucy Fitch Perkins
Lucy Maud Montgomery
Luther Benson
Lydia Miller Middleton
Lyndon Orr
M. Corvus
M. H. Adams
Margaret E. Sangster
Margret Howth
Margaret Vandercook
Margaret W. Hungerford
Margret Penrose
Maria Edgeworth
Maria Thompson Daviess
Mariano Azuela
Marion Polk Angellotti
Mark Overton
Mark Twain
Mary Austin
Mary Catherine Crowley
Mary Cole
Mary Hastings Bradley
Mary Roberts Rinehart
Mary Rowlandson
M. Wollstonecraft Shelley
Maud Lindsay
Max Beerbohm
Myra Kelly
Nathaniel Hawthrone
Nicolo Machiavelli
O. F. Walton
Oscar Wilde

Owen Johnson
P.G. Wodehouse
Paul and Mabel Thorne
Paul G. Tomlinson
Paul Severing
Percy Brebner
Percy Keese Fitzhugh
Peter B. Kyne
Plato
Quincy Allen
R. Derby Holmes
R. L. Stevenson
R. S. Ball
Rabindranath Tagore
Rahul Alvares
Ralph Bonehill
Ralph Henry Barbour
Ralph Victor
Ralph Waldo Emmerson
Rene Descartes
Ray Cummings
Rex Beach
Rex E. Beach
Richard Harding Davis
Richard Jefferies
Richard Le Gallienne
Robert Barr
Robert Frost
Robert Gordon Anderson
Robert L. Drake
Robert Lansing
Robert Lynd
Robert Michael Ballantyne
Robert W. Chambers
Rosa Nouchette Carey
Rudyard Kipling
Saint Augustine
Samuel B. Allison
Samuel Hopkins Adams
Sarah Bernhardt
Sarah C. Hallowell
Selma Lagerlof
Sherwood Anderson
Sigmund Freud
Standish O'Grady
Stanley Weyman
Stella Benson
Stella M. Francis

Stephen Crane
Stewart Edward White
Stijn Streuvels
Swami Abhedananda
Swami Parmananda
T. S. Ackland
T. S. Arthur
The Princess Der Ling
Thomas A. Janvier
Thomas A Kempis
Thomas Anderton
Thomas Bailey Aldrich
Thomas Bulfinch
Thomas De Quincey
Thomas Dixon
Thomas H. Huxley
Thomas Hardy
Thomas More
Thornton W. Burgess
U. S. Grant
Upton Sinclair
Valentine Williams
Various Authors
Vaughan Kester
Victor Appleton
Victor G. Durham
Victoria Cross
Virginia Woolf
Wadsworth Camp
Walter Camp
Walter Scott
Washington Irving
Wilbur Lawton
Wilkie Collins
Willa Cather
Willard F. Baker
William Dean Howells
William le Queux
W. Makepeace Thackeray
William W. Walter
William Shakespeare
Winston Churchill
Yei Theodora Ozaki
Yogi Ramacharaka
Young E. Allison
Zane Grey